INSPIRED BY LOVE

WORDS FROM THE HEART OF WOMEN

INSPIRED BY LOVE

WORDS FROM THE HEART OF WOMEN

By
Dawn M. Harvey
With Seven Women of Greatness

© Copyright 2018 Dawn M. Harvey

All rights reserved. This book is protected under the copyright laws of the United States of America. No portion of this book may be reproduced in any form, without the written permission of the publisher. Permission granted on request.

Published by:
Unlock Publishing House
6715 Suitland Road
Morningside, MD 2746
www.maximizedprodiuction.com

Scripture quotations taken from the Amplified® Bible, Copyright © 1954, 1958, 1962, 1964, 1965, 1987 by The Lockman Foundation. Used by permission. All rights reserved.

Scripture taken from the New King James Version. Copyright © 1982 By Thomas Nelson, Inc. Used by permission. All rights reserved.

Scripture quotations are taken from the Holy Bible, New Living Translation, Copyright © 1996, 2004. Used by permission of Tyndale House Publishers, Inc., Wheaton, Illinois 60189. All rights reserved.

Scripture taken from the Holy Bible, New International Version®. Copyright © 1973, 1978, 1984 International Bible Society. Used by permission of Zondervan. All rights reserved.

ISBN 13/ 978-1-7327503-2-6

Printed in the United States of America May 2018

Acknowledgments

This book is dedicated to love, for everything that it taught us and all that we were blessed enough to learn.

Contents

THE STRENGTH TO LOVE AGAIN 11
HELPMEET, I DON'T THINK SO! 31
YOU ARE ENOUGH 53
LEARNING TO LOVE 80
THE WRIGHT KIND OF LOVE 97
OVERCOMING THE STRONGHOLD OF DEPRESSION 138
THE FIGHT 157
PRAYING FOR YOUR SPOUSE 184

Foreword

Over the years I have heard so many people talk about the impact that love has had on them or the hurt that they have experienced from love. Some of them recovered quickly, some of them recovered slowly, and some of them never recovered at all.

Love in itself is a marvelous thing until you add people to the equation. It sounds funny, but love is pure and fluid. It flows through countless lives hoping to find a place to live. We as people may have the best of intentions, but because we are all different, we handle each other based on what we have learned and who we have become. Life molds our views, our values, our decisions, our goals and our methods. So unintentional or not we could at some point, mishandle love.

On the other hand, there are those of us who have mastered selflessness and acceptance. We have dealt with our own issues and now enjoy the results of our growth and development in spite of what we have been through. We now enjoy love.

I hope that with the stories and information you find here, it will simplify your process and help you obtain what you truly desire on this unavoidable journey called love. I pray that you enjoy this collaboration. I have kept it near and dear to me so that when it was time I could present it to you; from my heart to yours.....

~ Dawn M. Harvey ~ *Pastor, Author, Entrepreneur*

THE STRENGTH TO LOVE AGAIN

Dawn M. Harvey

INSPIRED BY LOVE

Where Does Love Begin?

I am from a very sensitive family background and dynamic. Like a lot of other families we've had our challenges, ups and downs, and obstacles to overcome. As a young girl I was diagnosed with cancer and as a result I struggled much of my adolescence which is probably hard to believe given the type of work that I have been blessed to do for over 30 years.

Transitioning from a child to an adult is already a very difficult process. Our body begins to change, and sometimes that process causes insecurities or personal issues. You're learning more about life and research indicates we often don't understand the impact of the affects the adolescent transformation has on our psychological and brain development until a certain age. We make mistakes along the way (*at least that is the answer we utilize when we are children and not quite sure how to spin that as we transition to adulthood.*)

All these things are pretty normal as it pertains to development and maturity. But on top of that, a terminal illness can be quite a challenge for a 15 year old. I am so grateful now for the empathy and compassion that I have for others as a result of the things I have suffered. Not to the point of regret but honestly to the point of gratitude.

INSPIRED BY LOVE

You might say, *"What does this have to do with Love?"* That is a great question. This is partially why this book exists. I'm going to talk to you about my viewpoint on being open to loving again in relationships that result in marriages, rewarding friendships with other people and re-establishing vibrant relationships with our family members. How do we begin to open our hearts again after life circumstances have left us feeling wounded, broken and apprehensive about engaging vulnerably in meaningful ways? I will discuss how you become sound enough to remain open to love after you encounter traumatic life experiences. My honest opinion is that the love of God transcends time, transforms lives, heals and resolves wounded hearts.

What I've discovered about love is that it starts somewhere. Babies experience it from their parents or the lack there of. We see it in terms of endearment through movies and television, or we experience it when we encounter other people as they interact with each other. These are all visual perceptions that shape our definition of what love looks like to us. Those are the things seen with our eyes, our vision. What about the love that can only be felt in our hearts. I believe that love comes from God. I believe that God's love gives us peace and brings us comfort. I believe that it directs and protects us. I believe that the love of God gives you a chance at life. Once we discover that greater exists beyond this cold, calculating and cruel world that we see or experience, everything changes. We can now embrace who God made us to be. This is what happened for me.

With everything that happened around and to me, I realized that God loved me. Recognizing God loved me, I could do anything and everything that He equipped me to do. This truth made me not rely on the love of people as we are human and we change our mind. Instead, it taught me to appreciate the real love that I experienced with people. I learned to appreciate their authenticity, their character and integrity as it pertains to having a relationship with me. This appreciation caused me to value relationships versus being dependent upon them. I think that love teaches us lessons that nothing else can. Love causes reflection and increases the power to be able to have compassion toward someone who hurt you and even pray for your enemies. The Bible tells us in the book of *Song of Solomon 8:6* that love is stronger than death and jealousy is cruel as the grave. If love is stronger than death then that would explain to us why the love of God can awaken things and restore us. When we as people truly love each other we can help someone who is depressed come back to life. Love is stronger than the most terrible thing that we experience.

INSPIRED BY LOVE

In essence, our view of love is all about perception. It is important that we don't see people as the source of our love but rather the instruments that God uses to display what love looks like in the natural. We must rely on God as our source for love, and that relationship with Him is primary. Our relationship with him spills over into every area of our lives. The moment I understand the source of love, what makes people yield, what makes people surrender and what can transform the heart of an angry or broken person I know that this serves as my guide all the days of my life.

I am very passionate about anything I believe in. If you are not governed by something, you are ruled by everything. I'm so glad that I found the love of God which directs me in the course of my life and serves as the basis for all of my decisions.

As we go into my perception and philosophy about relationships I want you to keep in the back of your mind that this book was written because I believe that God loves us and if God loves us then we are already enough. As we meet people and develop friendships or romantic relationships with them we come 100% certified by God. He has already given us His stamp of approval. This takes the pressure off of our expectations of the relationship because no one else can complete us. The authors of this book share this ideology. I saw their lives and I believe in them. I pray that you also glean from the words that they pinned on paper for you. I believe love caused them to be transparent so you may move quickly through assessing opportunities to give and receive love. With God being centric in our mind and a heart filled with expectation let's talk about love.

There is a current that flows through the lives of all people. It precedes the first conversation ever spoken, and it is desired by all that breathe. It is the universal rhythm that flows in and out of every human being. It is the rhythm of LOVE; the intent of it healing some, and the misuse of it destroying others. Love is more valuable than all it encounters. May True, Unhindered Love find and keep you.

The most amazing experience in the world is when a person finds true love. You experience butterflies when you are in contact with each other, and the high anticipation of what the two of you are about to encounter together can be overwhelming. We find glimpses of what love looks like, in and throughout our young and adult lives.

Imagine walking through a park; and as you stroll along, you pass a couple in the park gazing at each other as if no one else was there – except the two of them – when in reality, they have the company of many. And the love that they share is evident in the look you see them exchange.

INSPIRED BY LOVE

What about a restaurant that you visited with your parents as a child, and you watched your mother's eyes well up as she witnessed a man get down on one knee and propose to the woman he loved. You look back and forth between your mother and the couple across the room, taking in the emotions that her face expressed, then to the man who looked overjoyed but extremely nervous as he recited what seemed to take him forever to say, and finally the bride to be as she looked surprised, happy and so in love with her beau. It was like the entire restaurant stopped to witness true love. How amazing is it that everyone had an opportunity to witness what is suggested to be a "couples forever."

And then we've witnessed the love that hurts and causes grief. Love is not the culprit in itself, but the power of love grants pain access to our hearts. Ultimately it is people who cause pain and hurt. The issue is that if we did not love them, what they did would not matter. That is why so many people decide to never love again.

Imagine the tears of a woman breaking up with her man. She is sitting very still on the same bench in the park where a proposal took place for someone else years before, sharing that she just did not feel the same way that she did in the past. He is so confused. He loved her. He was satisfied. Why wasn't he enough for her? But the truth was that she loved him, she just didn't want to get married. As the tears stream down her face, you can see the mixed emotions of pain and relief. As he places his face in his hands, she gets up and walks away – never looking back. He just sits there, remembering that he had chosen her. This was the first time he had settled down. The other women did not mean anything, but HER! She had become his forever. He starts to second guess himself; questioning every move that he made, only to find no answers.

We see all of these different scenarios that mold what we think about love and how it makes us feel. We take what we experience in our personal environment as children and every encounter we have with all the acts of love that we see day to day, good or bad. And then, as we stroll through life, we collide with the person that we are to spend the rest of our lives with.

But, what happens when that loves fails? The euphoria of love translates into its cohabitants, pain, and grief. It can be such an amazing experience; or, a cycle of continued heartbreak. We can only hope that when you meet the love of your life, the love you share is enough.

I hope that here in this book, you find some words or strategies that allow you not to give up on love. That these words allow you to not only heal from that which brings tears to your eyes but helps you to love again. It takes strength to love again. It takes courage and certainty about who you are and that you have value. "Personal" value and

"Relationship" value Relationships complement us, but they should not define us. They mold us and develop us, but we should know who we are regardless of if we are in a relationship, or if we are alone. It is alone where you can make the necessary adjustments to love and be lovable. It is with ourselves that we must come to terms with who we really are. Selfish, loyal, happy, depressed, sad, angry and so on.

Once we come to terms with who we truly are, what we really want and what we have to offer, everything else flows. It allows you to sort through people and the information that they offer you faster. It allows you to be extremely honest with yourself about what's real and what's not. The older we get, the more we mature, the more we realize that we just do not have time to waste. And when you are mature enough to take ownership of your life and evaluate who people really are, you do not even have the energy to waste anyone else's time.

So, after all of the past relationships, life lessons, and personal experiences – how do you muster up the courage to love again? Think about what you have to sacrifice in order to have a healthy relationship. When you truly love someone, you work your way through their flaws and their issues. You expose yourself to them at the most vulnerable level, and you trust that this person will handle you with care and always be there. Their mistakes may look like attacks, and their weaknesses may not look like love. But, when you make a decision to love, really love; you find a way. You find a way to communicate, share and forgive. You find a way to trust, resolve and even fight fair. I guess what I am saying is –love always finds a way.

Maybe you have been hurt one too many times, and you've made up your mind to never love again. And you've postured your heart to just accept that it is not going to happen for you. But you start reading, working on yourself and maturing; and then some kind of way, love finds you in a coffee shop, at church or out with your friends – and there is nothing that you can do about it.

There is a song that goes:

How did you get here Nobody's supposed to be here
I tried that love thing for the last time
My heart says "No, no." Nobody's supposed to be here
But you came along and changed my mind.

And THAT is what love does. It keeps coming after you until it gets it right. Until it changes your mind. But, you are the only one who can decide to give love another chance. It takes strength and courage to press through the reality of pain from your past. It takes strength to give, trust and commit to someone again. And, it also takes understanding. An understanding of how to work through the process of loving again. How does love happen, and how can you maneuver through it and find what you truly want? Let's try to identify this process together and look at the phases of finding true love.

1. **The Choice**. This is when you encounter someone, and you determine if they are your type. There are so many types:
   - Body Shape
   - Style of Dress
   - Conversation
   - Interests
   - Reminds You of Someone
   - Intellect

   And the list goes on.
2. **Once you determine if someone is your type, then you decide if they are a fit.** Are you curious about the difference? A TYPE is what attracts you to someone; a FIT is what establishes a connection between you and that person. Strangely enough, this step is often missed or realized too late. We think because they are our type that means that they fit; and, that is not always true. They can have the figure or intellect that you desire, but they may not be family-oriented, or business-minded. So, they are sure enough your type, and you are super attracted

to them, and so you set out to make it work; only to find out six months down the road, that they were not a fit.

3. **Making a decision to commit to each other.** This is a verbal, well-thought-out conversation where the two of you verbalize your commitment to each other and what that means to both of you. You want to know each other's definition of commitment because everyone has had different experiences. So, that definition could easily be different. And, if you are not sure what the word "commitment" means to both of you, there are sure to be some major hiccups along the way. Make sure that you have clarity before you end that conversation with the one you love, and that your commitment is clearly defined.

4. **Enjoying the Romance.** This could also be number three; so, you may want to just flow as things happen. This is the so-called "honeymoon stage" of the relationship. Everything is cute, fun and wonderful. He / she can do no wrong; and, you simply cannot wait to see, hear or touch them again. Some people find the key to this stage, and it never wears off – others transition to the next phase.

5. **True Love.** The romance is, so to speak, over; and, you have seen each other's bad habits and flaws – and you still cannot live without each other. There

are spurts of romance and days of reality; but, you would not have it any other way. You just love them, exactly the way they are.

A lot of relationships end during the romance phase. They begin to see the habits and traits of the person that they are so infatuated with. Issues can interrupt romance; so if the two people are not committed to each other, they slide right out of the romance phase. If you look back over your relationships, you have probably seen these same patterns in your own dating / relationship history. Something happens to make the other person upset, and because it is merely romance and not a commitment, it is easy to walk away.

One of the things that has made this process easier for me is phase 2. The fit. Before we become emotionally attached, let's find out if we should be together in the first place. So often we are led by our feelings – which we need – but, if it is not going to align with the rest of your life, if it does not look like your "Relationship End Game," or if you cannot see yourself living with them for the rest of your life, unless they change; it is not a fit. You can love them All Day and Night, but it will probably end, and usually cause some kind of damage. If you secure and evaluate the fit first, I believe you will have a better chance of making it through the other phases because you will have determined that it is worth it.

When we are introduced to a relationship that lines up with our destiny, we find ourselves in a beautiful, yet unique, place at the same time. The things that we've experienced draw us closer together and allow us to appreciate each other more. But, the enemy uses the exact things that we've experienced to come after what we feel, what we want and what we believe. He's hoping that instead of our experiences being a blessing to us that they would cancel each other out and devour our hope in love and relationships. But God has spoken, and He is standing in the midst of His plan for our lives, promising to finish what He started.

God is our rear guard, according to *Isaiah 58:8*, and as we move forward in His plan for our lives, He wars against anything that would come up behind us to attack or distract us, including our past. So, my hope is in Him, and my humanness, my frailties nor my past have permission to steal or govern over my future. That is why I believe that having a prayer life is so important. It helps us maneuver through our emotions and the pain from our past. Prayer ushers in the sweet presence of God that brings us peace and assurance in Him and what is to come.

So, allow me to submit to you in closing that as much as we want our lives fulfilled, professionally, and, otherwise, as much as our heart's desire is happiness and healthy relationships. Be aware, too, that prayer prepares you for what you desire, it produces what you want, and it protects what you obtain. Even though this chapter is about the ability and courage to love again, I believe that the power to do so is in prayer. Because in prayer, is where you find yourself and discover the truth about others. It is where you hear and sense God moving in your heart and your head, directing your thoughts and helping you to process your emotions. Prayer is where strategy is birthed, and plots against you are dismantled. Prayer is where you experience the love of God and learn to love again.

    This chapter does not answer all of the nuances of love and romance. But I do hope that, at the very least, it encourages you to give love another try. Time, heartbreak and disappointment will not prevail on this journey to happiness. I am a firm believer that you can be amazing – alone. That relationships do not define us, but they sure do complement and support us. So, no, you do not have to be in a relationship to live an incredible life; but, if by chance you decide to give TRUE love another chance, I would like to think that these tools can be a part of your filtering process and save you time and heartache. Life has no guarantees, but it is still, regardless of your past or pain, filled with opportunity. I hope that you find your "FIT" and that "True Love" will wrap its arms around you.

INSPIRED BY LOVE

Now, allow me to introduce to you a group of women that I believe will help you overcome that which hinders you. May their words transform your mindset and your life. Happy reading…..DH

INSPIRED BY LOVE

Pastor Dawn Harvey's life's work is to Minister to, restore and develop the greatness in every person she encounters.

Operating in evidentiary gifts, Pastor Dawn strives to fulfill the call on her life by teaching, ministering, training and developing those that God has assigned, saved and winning the unsaved. She has a burning desire to win souls and annihilate the spirit of defeat. To preach God's saving grace and disciple others to do the same.

Pastor Harvey has a heart for people. She is no stranger to the challenges and the struggles of life. At 15, she was diagnosed with uterine cancer. Although she was given a grim prognosis, she miraculously survived the surgery and went into remission. A few months later, the cancer returned in one of her lungs; and, by the time she was transferred to Duke University Medical Center, it had spread to her brain. It is her sincere belief that God healed her and saved her life. With that in mind, she is simply driven to make a difference and have an impact wherever God places her.

As a corporate and leadership trainer, she has repeatedly proven her ability to develop, enhance and improve not only corporations and non-profit organizations, but entrepreneurs, ministries, and individuals, as well. She has a proven track record in the implementation and strategic development vital to yielding impressive results.

What drives Pastor Dawn Harvey is the possibility that ANYONE... ANYTIME... ANYWHERE... can make a decision to INCREASE their capacity and MAXIMIZE their life REGARDLESS of their current circumstances.

Pastor Dawn Harvey is a dedicated mother, a devoted friend and a consummate professional with over 25 years of corporate and professional experience. She was worked with notable companies such as Boddie Noell Enterprises, Marriott, Federal Express, Legal Shield, Dept. of Health and Human Services, Dept. of Transportation, HCD Inc., WSSC, etc. She the author of seven books and obtained her Doctorate of Christian Theology, in August 2015.

INSPIRED BY LOVE

Currently, her company offers management, branding and publishing services as she continues to also minister, approaching her twelfth year as Senior Pastor of DICC.

> "**You are destined for greatness, designed with a unique purpose, and covered with the anointing of God.**"
> ~ Dawn M. Harvey

HELPMEET, I DON'T THINK SO!

*"Helping Women Embrace Their Role As
A Help Meet With Happiness"*

Vonda Taplin

Let me begin with this declaration:

*S*ister, **YOU ARE STRONG!**

*G*irl, **YOU ARE GIFTED!**

*W*oman, **YOU ARE WEALTHY!**

*L*ady, **GOD LOVES YOU!**

I believe it is essential that every woman make a conscience decision to embrace God's truth of His thoughts toward her. ***"For I know the thoughts that I think toward you, saith the LORD, thoughts of peace, and not of evil, to give you an expected end"***. *Jeremiah 29:11.* My heart burns with Holy Spirit passion to empower and see women emotionally, psychologically, and spiritually healthy. My personal journey has taught me the importance of understanding God's thoughts concerning us and the mental havoc that is produced when we don't address our identity in Christ. I encountered an identity crisis orchestrated by satan that inflicted my soul. It turned out to be a blessing. My personal encounter with the Holy Spirit did not happen at a local church house. I was born again on May 15, 1995. I worked as a clerk at the Society Prevention for Cruelty to Animals (LaSPCA). As I was going about my responsibility as a clerk; I was filing papers; then suddenly, instantly and unexpectedly **God delivered me**. *<u>Yes! I said, suddenly, instantly and unexpectedly</u>*!

INSPIRED BY LOVE

God healed my wounded heart, poured his Love on me, changed my life and anointed me with the "Oil of Gladness". By now you're probably wondering why I'm sharing this with you. Well, I'm glad you asked. Although, my experience with God was absolutely divine, the "residue" of Satan's lies, the rejection, the insecurities, and the low estimation of how I viewed my own self-worth remained in my soul. As a result, the sweet hunger and thirst for my heavenly Father began, and it's GOOD.

God then called me to teach other women about how to live free in Jesus. More than anything I love to teach women on the character of God, and how we should do our very best to honor God with our conduct, character and conversation. My mission is to help women love themselves, learn more about God and His Son Jesus Christ and build loving and lasting relationship with others. Mostly importantly my friend, God will fulfill his purpose in you. *"Blessed is she who believed that the Lord would fulfill His promises to her." Luke 1:45*

My heart is to always encourage women to be their best selves and when we talk about marriage that can be complicated. Those who know me understand the way I communicate but since we probably have not met, I hope that you hear my heart in these pages and know that I want to save you some of the growing pains that I went through.
If you are like me, you probably wondered what it meant to become someone's "helpmeet." When I got married, I knew how to cook and clean; but, I knew nothing about

being a "helpmeet." Actually, I didn't even like the term "helpmeet." In my mind at the age of twenty-three, when I married, it sounded like a term used to describe a woman of no value. So naturally, I rebelled against what I didn't understand. Strong male domination was the norm in the environment, whereby, my beliefs were established.

Although my mother tried her very best to shield our eyes and mind from the negative influences of evil. In spite of all her efforts, relentless evil had wormed its way into my innocent thoughts. My thinking was contaminated by fear, shame, guilt, condemnation, and insecurity - to name a few. Hence, I made a decision that I would protect me from pain. I had already made up my mind that all men were the same. I saw men as mean, unloving, controlling, and always wanting to be "in charge" of the wife. As if she had no mind of her own. I was so limited and wounded in my thinking towards men; it resulted in me having a tormenting fear of men. I thought it was impossible for a man to express tender love and care towards women. I actually thought God created the male - to be controlling, mean, admittedly with an unaffectionate personality. In my wounded soul, I believed his primary and only purpose was to work hard; make sure the money was available to pay the bills; buy Christmas toys; birthday gifts; lavishly entertain guest; and, impress the neighbors; so he could feel a sense of accomplishment. Sadly, I believed the wife's role was to submit to his stern godliness personality.

INSPIRED BY LOVE

In addition, I was not going to be that type of helpmeet! I'm sure you can tell, by now, my dear husband had his work cut-out.

As you can tell, thus far, I did not know God as a loving Father. But, God gave me a loving, affectionate, sincere and good-looking man. Although, the enemy had wormed his way into my thinking about men. My husband's gentle charm navigated its way into the hurting girl in me, and he gained access to a door that had been locked for years. Actually, he had the keys. At a young age, I decided to close the door, because of rejection, pain, shame, and fear. However, my husband's love discovered what I had tucked away safely - my hopes, my dreams, my laughter, my confidence, and so many more hidden treasures. **I'm so glad God gave me my husband!**

By now, I want you to understand my reason for sharing some of what I had believed about men. My prayer is that you'll be able to recognize the strategic plan of the enemy who aims to destroy your future and your marriage. Come on sisters, open your eyes and see! Satan, cunningly, creeps his way into our minds so he can persuade us to believe his bad news. Yes, bad news – that dampens our joy, steals our gifts, and discourages our faith in God. Our enemy thrives on destroying good relationships and confident personalities. He is a defeated foe; and, he hates our obedience to God. I hope to make you aware of what

God has declared over you when He said, it's not good for man to be alone, I will make him a helpmeet.

If I had an understanding of the real meaning of the term "helpmeet" earlier in my life, my role and mission as a wife would have been more rewarding for my husband. God made me suitable and compatible with my husband. However, there were times in our relationship when neither of us appreciated and respected our unique differences. God called my husband into ministry shortly after we were married – I was not excited about that assignment. Because I did not sign-up to be the wife of a preacher! I was a comfortable carnal Christian, and a preacher-husband would challenge my comfortable religious training. God's call to my husband was the seminal moment of my profound healing. God had to teach him how to love me – he had married a woman with a pleasing appearance but a damaged soul. We dated three years, so he was not entirely oblivious to my insecurities. He loved, and felt he could rescue me from the pain of my past. After all, he was a collegiate football scholarship recipient; therefore, he believed he possessed a power to help me heal.

However, the task was higher than what he could accomplish alone. My insecurities provoked in him undisciplined emotions that created a hostile atmosphere. A long time ago when we argued, we had no discretion and no rules. We did not respect each other and dishonored our promise to God – we agreed before God to love, honor, obey, and respect one another. Bad enough we were financially broke – we had self-inflicted wounds; we were negative thinkers; our divine love laid dormant within our broken unrestored and unrestrained souls. We had no clue of how to make it better. We could not live with each other; and, did not want to live without each other. As I stated previously – being a preacher's wife was not a part of my agenda. I wanted to be "of" the world, not just "in" the world. Based on my perception, the people in the world seemed happier. The few preacher's wives I had been exposed to did not seem very happy or joyous. Many of them seem to be sad – just waiting to go to Heaven. I wanted to have fun on earth. I had a twisted view of the helpmeet role; partly because of what I saw in and out of the church. However, I'm grateful because the church is where I came to know and accept Jesus as my Lord and Savior. The seed of faith planted in my soul during my little girl years at Sunday school, and Vacation Bible School, shielded me during the times I felt alone and abandoned. After getting married, I realized the enemy had set up shop in my mind. Satan thrives on tormenting people with past failures, past mistakes, past sins, or whatever he can use to prevent you from an abundant life. I thought something was wrong with me; and saw no way out of the tormenting voices of my past.

Fortunately, during those times when the enemy pulled on the strings of my heart, I knew I had married a man that loves me with all his might. If you are not married, embrace God's love expressed in Jesus. The love of God is so powerful – it heals, delivers, and sets us free from sin.

God empowered my husband with divine, supernatural, unexplainable, and unconditional love. My husband fell in love with God and saw a better life with me as a whole woman. My husband had on the canvas of his spiritual imagination what he needed me to become as his wife; and, his love empowered me to complement his God-given assignment. I remember my husband telling me,

"An overly, insecure woman is unattractive and a hindrance to any confident man's productivity." Those words, spoken to me, turned the light on in my soul, and I saw the power of real love.

I had to decide to rise from the ashes and take my place in Christ. For too long, I gave Satan access to my soul, poisoned by the root of offense. ***I decided*** to forgive the people that hurt me, intentionally and unintentionally, and I took my life back. When I consider the agonizing pain my Savior Jesus Christ suffered for my liberty, I refuse to let what Jesus accomplished for me be wasted. I prayed to God to restore my soul so that I could be a happy woman – a woman of peace and helpful helpmeet. I no longer put the pressure on my husband to make me feel good about myself. Yes, I admit there were times when I did, and he tried. Honestly, your husband does not want that overbearing responsibility, it's too hard. I praise God that I'm no longer dominated by the bondage of fear, unforgiveness, insecurity, and other sabotaging negative emotions that held me in darkness and defeat. I boldly and purposely declare over my life daily, "the precious blood of Jesus has graciously written on my soul "access denied" to Satan."

My Journey to Healing:
AN UNPLANNED SHIFT

On Friday, August 26, 2005, it was another day of work and preparing for the weekend. My routine would help my husband with preparing for worship services, such as what worship song we'll sing, announcements to be made, and other logistics necessary for a fantastic worship experience. Our lives revolved around ministry and, maybe, in an unhealthy way. We both worked full-time jobs, and we, equally, shared the responsibility of supporting our sons, caring for our home, and ministering to the souls of men – as we struggled to like each other; because, our marriage was not on our list of things to do.

The weekend of August 26, 2005, was not a regular weekend for those living in the city of New Orleans and surrounding parishes. However, Sunday, as usual, for us never came. We experienced the devastating effect of Hurricane Katrina. We were ordered to evacuate the city, and we did. My husband and I canceled service and headed for higher ground. We traveled in a caravan with other family members, our sons, our parents, and my siblings – who were visiting for the weekend. We, initially, moved about 120 miles away from the hurricane, so that the return to the city would be quick after the hurricane passed. However, the return, as we imagined, never happened; 80 percent of the city was inundated by the floodwaters of Hurricane Katrina. As a result, we were not allowed back into the city; and, the closest and safest place we had to land was with relatives in Virginia. Finally, after three days of hard-pressed traveled, we finally arrived in Virginia.

A few days after arriving in Virginia, my husband and I sat in a *Taco Bell* restaurant located at 4248 Dale Blvd, Dale City, VA, looking at each other, *yes looking at each other,* something we had not done in a very long time. Remember, we were busy with Church work. As we set there, trying to figure out how all this happened – no access to our home, loss of jobs, our son's schools, their friends and the ministry we founded – was all gone in one weekend. And honestly, a part of me rejoiced, because my soul was wounded and the routine of ministry had taken its toll on me, particularly. I did not know how to do ministry – apart from work and toiling – serving from a place of neediness. I had no peace; and, I believe, deep in the heart of my husband, he saw and acknowledged that brokenness in me, as we set and talked while eating our tacos. We decided to settle down in Virginia, at least for our sons. We needed to create normalcy for them, as much as possible; they both were in their adolescent years. We lived in Virginia for two years, and it was a time of total healing and restoration for me. My husband was hired to work in "Men's Shoes" at *Nordstrom* Department Store in Tyson's Corner, VA; and, I was a stay at home wife and mother. We regularly attended church at *Church on the Rock Ministries*, under the leadership of Pastor Joseph and Lady Cynthia Graham.

During the day while my husband was at work, I spent a lot of time with God, seeking His presence and His power. I would take daily walks near the woods where our apartment complex was located; and, I could feel God's presence and hear His voice. God knew that I lived in the bondage of guilt and condemnation because insecurity will make you see what is not true, lashing out and fighting the wrong culprit. I was saved, but my God, I had a whole lot of residue lingering in my soul. I did not know I was approved and accepted by God, the very reason He chose me was to love me and heal me. The words of *Romans 5* came alive in my soul as I sat down one day on a bench during my morning walk. I was once again apologizing to God because I remembered some of the crazy things I had done, and said, in disobedience. Suddenly, I got a revelation directly from the Holy Spirit that Jesus Christ had freely given me "PEACE WITH GOD." Immediately my soul rejoiced! Alone in the woods, it was me, the trees, and the birds rejoicing in the Lord that day. Consequently, I no longer live under Satan's lies of guilt, shame, and condemnation.

HELPMEET- That's Who God Called Her

Let's now take a good look at the term "helpmeet." **"And the LORD God said it's not good that the man should be alone; I will make him a helpmeet for him"** Genesis 2:18. According to the Bible at the time of creation, everything God made was good. The only thing God said was "not good" was for man to be alone. WOW! Therefore, I am humbled and honored that God ascribed such a powerful and rewarding assignment to me as a woman. My assignments as a wife were God's idea and not man's personal ideologies. The term "helpmeet" in Hebrew is *"ezer" it means to help, succor, and support.*

Retake a look at *Genesis 2:18*, after God said **"I would make him a helpmeet",** God began to bring forth animals out of the ground and permitted Adam to name each one; but, still no help was found for Adam, the man of God. Personally, I believe God did not want Adam to get it twisted, thinking an animal can be his helpmeet. So, after God allowed Adam to identify animals properly. "But still no help was found." Adam's wife came from Him, not the ground. God put Adam into a deep sleep; and, while Adam was sleeping – God took from Adam then added to Adam. Now that was deep. Creating his Good Thing! Moreover, she was opposite. God created her to be opposite. What a beautiful picture. Two people made of the same substance, different in role and functionality – fitting together – creating a complete picture. Adam's spirit and soul came straight from the breath of God. God only had to blow the breath of life into Adam's nostrils to bring his soul to life. Nowadays, the dynamics that influence the souls of men and women are different, *(those dynamics will be discussed in my next book)*. But, Adams soul was influenced by the spirit of God. I believe that's why Adam had the power of naming a thing, and it became whatever Adam called it. Adam was God's voice and vision in the earth. Adam said what God said, and Adam saw what God saw. One of my husband's strongest attributes is security and confidence. He is just wired that way. Yes, even before he was saved. Don't judge him, because he is now saved, secure and confident in Jesus – fueled by the Holy Ghost. Whoever or whatever we were in the world; God fills us with His love and uses those same strengths for Kingdom purposes.

So, being that my husband is a watchful man, he sees every slithering snake I see, and the ones I don't see! His watchfulness is not motivated by a lack of trust in my commitment, and we have been adultery free and faithfully in covenant with each other for nearly thirty years. The Bible declares that we be spiritually awake, watchful and sober-minded. *1 Thessalonians 5:6.* God formed me, but I needed my husband to speak words over me to restore my wounded soul. There were too many times in our marriage that neither of us understood the language of marriage. Yes, successful marriages have a harmonious sound. I'm going to share with you three healing benefits my husband's expression of love has done for my soul.

Happiness:
*** Happy is the man that findeth wisdom, and the man that getteth understanding.*** Proverbs 3:13

I'm a happy wife, and I choose to have a happy life. Godly wisdom is the key to a happy life. My happiness and my faith in God is the connector; the power source of my stability. So that I will not assume we all share the same perspective on how happiness is defined. I'm going to use the biblical definition of "happy" from *Proverbs 3:13* – the Hebrew word is (Esher – blessed, to make happy), the root word is (Asher – to set right, righten, to pronounce happy, call blessed). Then Leah said, "How happy I am! The women will call me happy." So, she named him Asher. *Genesis 30:13*. According to the *New Testament*, the Greek word for happy is (Makarios – blessed, happy). My soul is happy in Jesus; and, my husband is the benefactor of my relationship with Jesus. For a long time, I thought the outside stimulants could give me the source of happiness I craved. Although material things have its place, ultimately, I learned that God alone could fill the hole in my soul. The promise of happiness is in the word of God and transforming my mind to receive what God says is how I choose to live. Wisdom is essential, and it's the foundation of having a happy relationship.

I believe that women set the tone in the home. Her power of influence can build the house or tear it down. ***The wise woman builds her house, but with her own hands the foolish one tears hers down.*** *Proverbs 14.1.*

Consequently, her husband should know how to have a relationship with her beyond the bedroom. Her emotional stability is directly linked to his expression of love; therefore, dating, communicating and relating to her is the husband's responsibility. The Bible tells us that Adam was in a deep sleep when God created woman. Therefore, she was his mystery. Sometimes, as women, we are uncertain about what we want. Thus, husbands are encouraged to dwell with his wife with understanding. As a wife, my happiness is important to my husband; and, most of the time, he is not the cause of my emotional instability because those old memories sometimes get in my way. My husband and I both want a happy marriage, and we both share the same philosophy regarding our relationship. The bedrock of our happiness is our faith in Jesus Christ and our willingness to submit our words and actions to the authority of the Holy Spirit.

INSPIRED BY LOVE

His loves cultivate my health:
Gracious words are a honeycomb, sweet to the soul
and healing to the bones. *Proverbs 16:24*

I hate fussing. Moreover, whenever my husband and I argued, the use and tone of our words were not gracious. I've never been a person to use foul language, and that discretion was my practice even during our most heated disagreements. For this very reason, offensive and abusive words caused terrible memories to surface. And, I think we both just "got tired" of dishonoring each other and God. I just began to submit, totally, to the order of God regarding marriage. My husband takes his responsibility as a husband very seriously. He recognizes and acknowledges his role as a leader in our home. I respect and submit to his leadership because I trust him. He loves God, and he spends time with God. I believe in him, even when I'm not sure where he's going. I no longer fight against his leadership. He has an impeccable record of accomplishment as a man, a husband, a father and as my Pastor. My husband has never known his father, and his mother raised him. We have two sons, and they are the source of his joy. He survived the mean streets of the "hood" during his adolescent and young adult years. By the grace of God, he never fell prey to the trappings of alcohol, drugs, and the violence in the mean streets of the ghetto. I asked him how he survived and his confession continues to be, "I am a winner."

As a result, we have overcome personal and relationship challenges, and together we win. We both have a spiritual relationship with God and we understand the power of two.

Submitting To The Call:

[22]Wives, submit yourselves to your own husbands as you do to the Lord. [23]For the husband is head of the wife, just as Christ is the head of the church, His body, of which He is the Savior. Ephesians 5:22-23

I have worked as an Administrative Assistant for nearly 25 years. I have worked directly with the authority of *Hospital Directors* to *College Presidents*; and, I have never dishonored their position. Therefore, I decided to trust God, honor the authority of my covering, and submit to my calling as a wife. God has an already established order in the earth for marriage relationships, and it works. God told Adam, "I'm giving you some help on the earth." The woman's job is so powerful and her obedience to God's order will empower her to give birth to heaven on earth. Additionally, a woman's influence can bring deliverance or devastation. Adam was in partnership with the woman God created for Him. ***So, when the woman saw that the tree [was] good for food, that it [was] pleasant to the eyes, and*** *a tree desirable to make [one] wise, she took of its fruit and ate. She also gave to her husband with her, and he ate."*

"So when the woman saw that the tree [was] good for food, that it [was] pleasant to the eyes, and a tree desirable to make [one] wise, she took of its fruit and ate. She also gave to her husband with her, and he ate."

Eve's disobedience led to the fall of creation; and, women had a sentence passed on to them, subject to sorrow and subjection. She will be subject to an inherently distorted, dominate and insecure husband. "But God!!!" Jesus has restored our place in fellowship with God!! Hallelujah!!! *"And I will put enmity between you and the woman, and between your offspring and hers; he will crush your head, and you will strike his heel."* In *Genesis 3:15*, the sentence of sorrow and subjection is revoked for the wife who put her hope in Jesus. She can fulfill her role as a wife and mother with love and happiness. I believe my healing was my husband's first kingdom assignment, and he took it seriously. *"Husbands, likewise, dwell with them with understanding, giving honor to the wife, as to the weaker vessel, and as being heirs together of the grace of life, that your prayers may not be hindered."* 1Peter 3:7

Most of the time, my husband embraced God's command to dwell with me according to knowledge. Certainly, there were times the calling was more than he desired. In spite of the challenges, our marriage relationship grew healthier and stronger. As I stated before, I try hard not make my emotional health my husband's responsibility. My desire is to be his good thing!!

HIS LOVE, MY HOLINESS

Husbands, love your wives, just as Christ loved the church and gave himself up for her to make her holy, cleansing her by the washing with water through the word, and to present her to himself as a radiant church, without stain or wrinkle or any other blemish, but holy and blameless.

One of my favorite scripture is *Matthew 5:8*: **"Blessed are the pure in heart, for they will see God."** I wanted to see God; not just when I get to heaven, but I longed to see him and know him while living in the earth. So, I knew that if I sought to have a clean heart before God, he would reveal himself to me. Therefore, I started my journey toward having a right heart before God. I know my assignment as a wife has the potential to influence the divine dynamics of our home. The Holy Spirit taught me how to be what my husband needed as his wife. The more I became who God made me, the clearer the vision of my husband's love became. My husband's expression of love to me is divine. Because my husband is a man of God, he learned how to love from where I was. He planted in me a deeper longing for God. As a result, my perspective of being his helpmeet was no longer as toiling task that I once despised. I'm humbled that God says, **"When a man finds a wife (me), he finds a good thing (me) and obtain favor from the Lord."** Proverbs 18:22. My calling is as a wife is from God; therefore, I do not take it presumptuously, and it is God's power working in me to be His preacher's wife. *To God be the Glory!* The heartbeat of a healthy marriage is rooted in the power of both husband and wife submitting to God, and a willingness to give into the needs and desires of one another. Consequently, submitting to the ways of God in marriage will protect the relationship from ungodly control and influence. Marriage is ordained by God to be the very reflection of Christ and the Church. My husband and I have not yet attained all that is meant to attain, but we find joy in pressing on. The mystery of love is ever increasing, forever learning, and forever giving.

My God-given assignment is to be the wife my man found, and fashioned, by the Power of God's love that he possesses. Who Can Find A Virtuous Woman?

INSPIRED BY LOVE

Pastor Vonda K. Taplin is a New Orleans native, Vonda serves diligently alongside her husband Pastor Anthony W. Taplin Sr. senior pastor of Come Into The Light Ministries in New Orleans, LA, an innovative and thriving ministry. Vonda's greatest joy is being the wife to her wonderful husband of twenty-nine years and the mother to their two awesome adult son's Anthony Jr. and Ashton.

Vonda is also the founder of W.I.C. Ministry (Women In Christ). A ministry designed to enlighten, encourage and equip women with spiritual and practical knowledge, thereby perfecting Godly Character while enjoying and living the Good Life. Her concern and compassion for hurting women & girls and the challenges that pursue them are the dynamics of her mission called H.A.G.A.R Mentoring Ministry (Helping Adolescent Girls Receive

Restoration). Vonda knows what it is to live with, YET OVERCOME; the deception of the enemy.

As a child and teenage Vonda nursed the wounds of She believes as the scripture says: ***"Therefore if any man be in Christ, he is a new creature: old things are passed away; behold all things are become new.*** *II Corinthians 7:15*

Vonda is the host Pastor for **G**lorious **R**estoration **of W**omen Empowerment Conference, her testimony of deliverance is the motivation of her calling to help hurting women get healed and **G.R.O.W.** in God's promises and purpose for the life.

Vonda's an ordained minister; an Alumna of Southern University at New Orleans where she earned a Bachelor of Sciences in Criminal Justice. She is the daughter of Rosetta & Wellmond Arcenaux Jr. she has four sisters and one brother.

YOU ARE ENOUGH

Diahann Smith

INSPIRED BY LOVE

"It's not who you are that holds you back, it's who you think you're not" **Jean-Michael Basquiat**

As a little girl growing up in Brooklyn, New York, my home was often filled with the aroma of my Jamaican Mama's stew chicken brewing and the TV playing in the background with her favorite shows: *I Love Lucy*, *The Jeffersons*, *All In The Family* and her soap operas, *All My Children*, *One Life to Live* and *General Hospital*. When Mama wasn't cooking, she could be found washing clothes and cleaning. Our evenings began with my Dad coming in from work, washing his hands while my Mom summoned all of my siblings and I to come to the dining table. Dad was home, and it was time to eat. Like most young girls of my generation, I played with Barbie and Ken dolls, my pink Suzie Homemaker oven, a doll house, and watched countless Disney movies with the same primary theme: a damsel in distress being rescued by her prince. In elementary school, I sang my first child's play love jingle, "Diahann and Jay sitting in a tree, K-I-S-S-I-N-G/ first come love, then come marriage/ then comes the baby in the baby carriage." I saw Cinderella getting swept off her feet by her knight in shining armor and just knew there would be a day when I, too, would be discovered by my prince.

I was raised in a household with parents who have been married for over forty-five years, so I never once entertained the notion that I would be walking life's journey as a single woman. Even in my earliest recollections, I saw marriage as a natural progression into adulthood. My parents' example made marriage attractive to me. I saw them as two adults who joined forces to raise a blended family of seven with the hope of offering their children a better life than the one they lived. For over forty-five years my Dad woke up at 4am every day and headed off to work. He was a welder and installed piping all throughout the New York tri-state area. My Mom would rise shortly after him and head down to the kitchen to turn on the tea kettle. Every morning, my parents sat down and had a cup of tea together before they started their day. It was normal for me to awaken to the sounds of a whistling tea kettle and my parents' morning dialogue. I have watched my parents navigate the many seasons of life. They put six children through college, in the midst of being teenage parents. They were adamant that all of us would graduate from college, so they devised a plan for the entire family to pitch in to take care of my nieces and nephews while my sisters went to school at night. We watched our parents endure significant struggle and loss: our brother Alvin died from lupus, my Dad losing his Mom while he battled cancer, Mom taking care of Dad, nursing him back to health, and them teaching our blended family how to co-exist in harmony. My parents were not exempt from the day-to-day fights, frailties, conflict, and heartbreak many relationships have to conquer in order to be successful.

However, I saw a committed partnership walking through both the expected and unexpected curve balls of life, and I wanted this type of partnership for myself. But what do you do when the life you desired is not your reality? What do you do when life changes suddenly and your happily ever after is tragically interrupted? What do you do when promises are broken, and you're left alone to pick up the pieces?

You are not alone. All of us have desires for the life we imagine as the ultimate plateau of our existence. Yet, life takes on many shapes and destinations we never thought would be part of our journey. We make plans; do our best, only to find that our path takes us elsewhere. Life is a series of events intended to get us to an expected end. We must be willing to let go of the life we planned in order to get to the life that will bring us true contentment. It is my intent to engage in a transparent conversation with the modern-day single about the issues we must face head on to live an authentic, happy existence in a society where the definition of 'traditional' is changing every day. Societal norms can be an enemy of personal liberty. Whatever state of singleness you find yourselves in today, you matter. Every individual has an impactful story. There is an audience with your name assigned to it. Every one of God's creations was created with an expected end in mind.

INSPIRED BY LOVE

Your existence wasn't your idea. God knew his purposes for you before you were conceived. Not one detail of your existence is coincidental. God sees you right where you are.

I share the truths I have learned in my journey with the hopes that through the gleaning of my life, you will gain the courage to step outside of the box of every definition of a traditional life that hinders you from embracing the grace that was carved out just for you. Grace, "the unmerited favor of God," birthed a capacity in you to become something to behold. This grace was intended to fulfill the earthly assignment only you can complete. There is a grace that is reserved for you which only flows freely when you come into alignment with the purpose for which the grace was given. There is a capacity buried within you that comes alive with the acceptance of the path you were set on. Webster's dictionary classifies acceptance as a noun and is defined as "the action of consenting to receive or undertake something offered" and "the action or process of being received as adequate or suitable." Acceptance breeds understanding. Much of the understanding we seek is buried under the despair of not wanting to be in the state we are in. When our hearts are consumed with the desire to escape a place rather than embrace it, we have just blocked our ability to receive the grace to overcome.

Acceptance breeds peace. Acceptance is the key that unlocks the answers that have already been placed within you. You're graced for your intended path. In your singleness, will you accept and abide in the grace which has been offered to you from a God that loves you. Will you accept God's choices for your life? It is my belief that we dismiss the power of the grace being offered to us in life situations because it's too simple to just receive. In a world that teaches you must earn everything you obtain, receiving grace seems incomprehensible. Grace can't be earned. There is nothing you can do to earn grace. Grace is freely given for you to prosper in whatever state and condition life has presented. It is a choice to abide in grace.

"And God is able to make all grace [every favor and earthly blessing] come in abundance to you, so that you may always [under all circumstances, regardless of the need] have complete self-sufficient in Him, and have abundance for every good work and act of charity.
2 Corinthians 9:8 (AMP)

Too many of us relinquish the grace that has already been offered to thrive in the space we find ourselves by putting constraints on our heart. Our heart conforms to the capacity we believe it will. When we believe we have the ability for a matter, our emotions and energy connect with the strength to perform it. Grace does not exist to be constrained. Grace cannot be manipulated. Grace is extended for us to flourish in our assigned places, not the place of our choosing. We stifle our capacity to flourish when we dismiss the value and dread the assigned places life has taken us.

Fulfillment only comes when we align our heart with the plan God orchestrated when he saw *"you were very good."* God examined everything he created and placed his stamp of approval on your existence. The Bible records in *Genesis 1: 31 (KJV)* ***"God saw all that he had made, and it was very good." God took a look at every aspect of who you are and yet to become and declared "you are very good."*** I have learned to abide in God's grace in my singleness, recognizing that being single is not the totality of my existence.

Dispel the notion that marriage is the end all to your happiness. When we put total emphasis on obtaining happiness from someone else and external things, we are chasing an illusion that our contentment is connected to forces beyond our control. When our happiness is directed externally, we will always be waiting for the next thing or person to show up to make us happy. When the external thing or person doesn't yield the expected happiness we assumed it would; we begin chasing something else. Our quest for happiness rooted in external things takes us on an emotional goose chase. First, our attention is focused on finding a house to make us happy, and then when the house begins to need repairs, then we move on to getting a new car to make us happy, When the car starts acting up, then we need our children to be perfect to be happy, and when the children start acting up, then we need the perfect person to show up and make us happy. When we put primary emphasis on our happiness being rooted in something and someone else we are saying, **"I am not enough."**

When you place your happiness in the hands of others, you will find yourself chasing after the wind, or just a false pursuit leading nowhere with any long-term fulfillment. Happiness is not a final destination. Happiness is an acceptance that life is an on-going journey full of a myriad of seasons of highs and lows that cannot be avoided. Happiness is choosing to thrive in spite of what we face. Happiness recognizes that we cannot protect ourselves from sadness without protecting ourselves from happiness. We willfully accept to completely engage in our journey, knowing happiness is available to us. Happiness wasn't meant to be elusive; it was meant to be discovered. Happiness requires our fundamental belief that it was meant for us. We must first believe we are worthy of happiness before it will be found.

At the root of your existence, you must know you were created to be happy. Happiness is your birthright. Happiness does not mean everything is perfect and we are void of challenges. Happiness is the abandonment of the notion that life was made to be perfect. Happiness is choosing to exist in a continual state of contentment despite the challenges we may face. Happiness trusts things will become beautiful in their own time. Happiness resides in optimism. Until we recognize we are the drivers of our happiness we will continue to place the burden of our happiness on others. Many of our relationships suffer because we are silently holding others accountable for our happiness. We place an unrealistic burden, a subconscious expectation that the other party is responsible for our happiness.

For the first time in American history, statistics indicate singles are the growing majority. According to the U.S. Census Bureau of Labor and Statistics, singles represents over 50% of the American population. In 2014, the Bureau of Labor Statistics reported that 124.6 million Americans 16 years and older were single, or 50.2 percent of the population, compared with 37.4 percent of the population in 1976. The Bureau of Labor Statistics has been tracking statistics for singles in America since 1976. When we consider the number of singles in America who have never been married, the percentage jumps to 63%.

It is important to note that this classification of single includes those that have been previously married and widowers.[1] Given the fact that singles are the new norm, it behooves us to make peace with the person and path that was created for us.

It is my belief that we only come into authentic happiness through fulfillment. Our definition of fulfillment is different for each of us based on our core values, cultural standards, and the belief systems we have adopted. Our core values are the principles, standards, and beliefs that we adopt that serve as our guideline for daily living.[2] Many of our core values are formulated and taught from as early as childhood. Our first encounter with understanding acceptable behavior and standards for living are instilled during our childhood.

As we gain our independence, we begin to alter our core values based on the perception of how we believe the instilled values have served us. My core values are a hybrid of my parents' silent generation and that of my own generation X. While I am disciplined, hardworking, fiercely loyal, and embrace traditional family values, I am also very resourceful, crave work/life balance, and an independent thinker. Coming from parents who came to America in the crux of a changing economy looking to escape the impoverished conditions of their home country of Jamaica,

---

[1] www.csmonitor.com/USA/.../Singles-nation-Why-so-many-Americans-are-unmarried
[2] https://www.reference.com/world-view/definition-human-values-3460c0b1f30ded9

INSPIRED BY LOVE

WI, and my parents taught us that college education was not an option; it was a necessity for survival. It seems like it was just yesterday my Mom was preparing my final bags getting ready to ship her baby girl off to college. As she stuffed my last items into my trunk, my Mom looked at me and said, "Diahann, you do not have to choose the life I chose for myself." These words served as encouragement on the many days when my life experiences did not mirror those of my Mom. I was headed upstate NY to study Communications at S.U.N.Y. at Fredonia. As a high school senior my English teacher recognized my gift with words and encouraged me to pursue Communications. I decided to take her recommendation as I've always had a love affair with words. College was life-changing for me. As most youngsters leaving home for the first time, I was excited about the idea of being on my own with no curfews and expecting to have a blast living out all the epic adventures you hear about college life. College provided me with an array of opportunities to explore my talents independently. It was my first experience learning how to coexist with cultures and ideologies different from my own perspective while staying true to my own convictions.

It also served as my first glimpse of seeing myself through the eyes of others up close. I was elected into leadership roles through my volunteer activities serving as a class representative for my Student Union and captain of our Step Team. The spotlight consistently found me as much as I tried to shy away from it. I was consistently being solicited to lead. I discovered my talents superseded my shyness. Passion drove me beyond my inhibitions. This would become the pattern of my life. My entire circle of college friends were first-generation college students. We left the concrete jungles of our inner cities determined that education was going to be our way out. We made a pact that no matter, what we would all graduate. We were an eclectic group of artistic beings who were able to find a healthy balance between partying, studying, volunteering and dating.

After four years of moments that changed us all forever, our entire crew graduated. Half of my circle married classmates they dated while in school. I wasn't focused on being in a serious relationship, as I thought I had plenty of time for that down the road. Besides, I was having too much fun with freedom. Being a sister of siblings who were teenage parents, I spent the majority of my preteen life helping to take care of my nieces.

Several years out of college, I would enter the relationship that threw me into my journey of self-discovery. I was in a relationship with someone who wanted to build a life with me, which was the catalyst that exposed my emptiness and how lost I felt. I wrestled with the idea that I should be ecstatic to have a good guy who wanted something real. Instead, the relationship alarmingly awakened my quest to understand who I was. I wondered how could I be entrusted with someone else's heart when my own heart was rumbling with so many questions. I didn't want to be rescued like the many messages Disney portrayed in my youth. I wanted to be a key contributor. I learned firsthand from my parents' example that marriage was about serving each other. How could I be a key contributor in any relationship without knowing what I had to offer? I was in the midst of a spiritual awakening and associated my worth with purpose. Until I could identify the root of this internal crisis, I needed to do the right thing, and I ended the relationship because it was not fair for me to put the burden of my happiness on someone else. I came to the decision that I would focus all my attention on figuring out this internal void why I felt this longing to do something different.

At the crux of this awakening, my twin sister Diana received a job offer in the Washington, DC area and she invited me to join her. My decision to join her pushed me head first into the plan of God. *Proverbs 19:21(AMP)* **Many plans are in a man's mind, But it is the Lord's purpose for him that will stand (be carried out).**

I had a plan for how I would establish myself in the DMV after we moved: As soon as Diana and I got settled, we would contact the headhunter who secured her job offer, and I would get a job in no time. We arrived in the DMV only to discover that the headhunter was missing in action. I ended up temping for over a year. While temping, I encountered many employers who treated temporary employees more like cattle than humans. This left a lasting impression on me. I vowed that when I got into a position of influence, I would treat people with compassion. I worked on a variety of temporary assignments which required me to work in different environments every day. As one who strived for stability, life was about to teach me how to thrive in constant change. I had to learn how to temper myself and remain grounded in environments that didn't appeal to my comfort zones. Learning to thrive in constant change would become necessary for my life's course. Temping didn't pay much, so I cut down commuting costs by walking for an hour going to and from the metro every day. I occupied myself by praying during my daily walks. My prayer moments began as a result of my being disappointed that the headhunter had disappeared. The daily walks became enjoyable as I forgot about my need for the headhunter to reappear and began just talking to the Lord. My need was no longer important as I focused on what God thought was important. God began to show me the needs of others in my prayer time. My heart became an incubator for the causes of God. This season was my introduction to intercession.

    After a year of prayer walks, the headhunter resurfaced. She contacted my sister saying she had a job that would be perfect for me. This job would be the opportunity that launched me into my career in Human Resources.

INSPIRED BY LOVE

Corporate America would become my training ground for cultivating purpose, revealing many of my gifts, and enabling me to teach individuals tools for identifying and connecting with their purpose. My career excelled as the pull to greater ministerial service and intercession intensified. Intercession would become a way of life for me. My life was taking on a path that I didn't plan. I started out this journey of self-discovery believing I was being prepared to be a great gift for one someday. Unbeknownst to me, I was being prepared to be a gift which would be offered to many. I have been very fortunate to have met several great men in my dating experiences over the years. While none have led to marriage, they each have exposed parts of myself that only surfaced when I chose to let another person in my intimate space. Relationships are a great teacher of self. Any opportunity to learn of yourself and gain the jewels offered only by authentic connections is worth it. Relationships are a gift. They offer us gifts of fulfillment and joy when we give them the liberty to blossom outside of our faulty expectations. We are relational beings driven by connection. Our perspective on relationships and what we believe we are entitled to directly impact their outcome. We are creatures of love. We were crafted out of love. Love is always beckoning. We miss it when we lose a pure perspective and attempt to regulate the vehicle and manner in which it presents itself.

INSPIRED BY LOVE

Oftentimes the very thing we seek is hindered by the weight of our expectations. We must remove every faulty expectation of what we think we are supposed to yield from an experience and merely choose to enjoy the gift of the relationship. Too many times we step into relationships with our broken history dictating what we will and won't do and don't recognize we've already crippled the purity of the connection. We constrain the liberty of authentic connection when we put pressure on them, as we attempt to control the outcome. You cannot control anyone's ability to love you. It is our responsibility to discern if the other party is capable of receiving and protecting our love. *"The truth is everyone is going to hurt you. "You have to find the one that you believe is worth suffering for." (Bob Marley).* Brokenness hinders many from receiving the very treasures they have asked for. I've learned there are moments we are offered as gifts to others as agents of healing. Some folks must encounter you to redefine their faulty definitions of love and acceptance. What a powerful notion, God entrusted your heart to be a safe landing place for someone else's restoration and recovery. Jesus is the ultimate illustration of being a love offering. We have allowed our romanticized perceptions of entitlement to hinder us from experiencing love in its purest form. Love at its purest form isn't self-seeking. It's offered. **"For God so loved the world that he gave his only begotten Son."** *John 3:16a (KJV).* We destroy relationships with our contaminated perspectives of entitlement. When we show up in our relationships entitled we are saying, "This relationship owes me for all the bad experiences I've allowed." The relationship is already at a deficit with our unspoken demands and faulty expectations. We typically assign emotional expectations based on the category we assign the individual (friend, spouse, colleague, acquaintance). The more emotional access and trust we decide to give the individual, the greater the expectations we hold them to. We tend to run into conflict when we assign emotional expectation to a relationship role that the individual has not agreed upon. For instance, we have made the decision this acquaintance is going to be my friend when the individual has deemed you an acquaintance. You deserve to be in relationships that make you happy, that feed your soul, and help you grow. You are worthy of connections that are loving, nourishing, kind and authentic. You deserve the love you keep trying to give everyone else. Before you can connect authentically with others, your connection with yourself must be authentic. Own your truth. Contentment requires honesty.

In my own moments of self-reflection, I recognized I was attempting to fit into a mold that didn't exist. I found liberty in unbecoming what I thought I needed to be and where I thought my path should have taken me. I recognized I didn't have to explain the grace on my life; I just had to live it. Make peace with your path.

INSPIRED BY LOVE

Acceptance breeds the liberty that is necessary to become. Make peace with your disappointments. When we do not face our hurts, they cripple us. We begin to view our world through the eyes of our disappointment. Disappointment is real. None of us are exempt from tragedy and crisis. Life will present us with experiences beyond our control. We can control how we choose to handle the experiences. I believe many hold on to disappointment for fear of being judged for how they truly feel, and they bury their pain. You cannot gain fulfillment living life through walls of disappointments. Disappointment steals our zeal to explore. A willingness to explore and take risks is necessary to find fulfillment. Life opens up one step at a time through our willingness to connect in spite of our pain. Life happens in the mist of our broken pieces. When we stay in a posture of disappointment for too long, we lose our will to overcome. We were built to overcome. The DNA of your origin is victorious. You are worthy of healing. You can't quit and win. Identify a support system that provides you emotional safety and begin the healing process. If where you are is overwhelming, seek help. Process the root of what is driving the disappointment and choose to heal. Choose to let go of the emotional attachments that are no longer serving you. If we truly believe the steps of a good man are ordered by the Lord, then we must recognize God is in control of this ordered place. I didn't choose this path; it chose me. *Psalm 37:32 (AMP)* states, **"The steps of a [good and righteous] man are directed and established by the Lord, And He delights in his way [and blesses his path]."** Making peace with your path requires you to settle the questions of a soul consumed with desire. I had to quiet the noise of a soul that wanted to dictate purpose. I dug deep and addressed the internal questions that most singles won't say aloud. Was my desire to be married based on the fear of being alone? Did my decision to focus on my thriving career cost me covenant? Was I going to grow old alone? Was I making my desire to be married an idol? Did I conquer enough character lessons to produce the level of integrity necessary to thrive in marriage? What is your motivation for wanting to be married? Is it rooted in God's original purpose for marriage or is your desire to be married based on a faulty expectation of an illusion of what you think marriage will solve for you? You have to be real with yourself and own the answers that come with your internal inventory. Our motivation for marriage should be rooted in its original purpose and not solely based on a romanticized ideal.

The bible outlines several scriptural purposes for marriage:
(1) Established the institution of family in the earth *(Genesis 1:27-28)*
(2) for man not to be alone *(Genesis 2:18)*
(3) for woman to serve as a helpmate to man *(2:18)*

- *(4)* As a model of Christ relationship with the Church *(Ephesians 5:21-33)*
- (5) to become one flesh *(Matthew 19:6)* Marriage is a God-ordained service ministry.

Marriage is an open illustration of Christ's relationship with his church. While addressing the church at Corinth the Apostle Paul responds to the Corinthian church questions concerning marriage and sexual morality as he specifies in *I Corinthians 7:7-8 (KJV)* ***"For I would that all men were even as I myself. But every man hath his proper gift of God, one after this manner, and another after that. I say therefore to the unmarried and widows, it is good for them if they abide even as I."*** Paul just identified the grace to remain single as a gift. How many singles truly see singleness as a gift? Jesus was single. Jesus's earthly ministry focused on preaching, teaching, healing, and performing miracles on his way to his purpose: to die on the cross. The bible lets us know Jesus is personally acquainted with the many emotions known to man. He wept *(I John 11:35)* was moved with compassion *(Matthew 14:14)* distressed *(I Luke 22:42)* and even sorrow and feelings of heaviness *(Matthew 14:34)*. It is my belief that Jesus left a witness for every experience we would face in this flesh. Jesus modeled the way for dealing with the rumblings of the soul: consistent prayer. Prayer centers our soul and its many cravings.

INSPIRED BY LOVE

Even God craved connection as he sought to commune with Adam and seeks to commune with us every day. Dr. Brene Brown, a Professor at the University Of Houston Graduate Of Social Work, while speaking on the conclusions derived from her research on social connections in an interview with Psychology Today, stated, "A deep sense of love and belonging is an irresistible need of all people. We are biologically, cognitively, physically, and spiritually wired to love, to be loved, and to belong. When those needs are not met, we don't function as we were meant to. We break. We fall apart. We numb. We ache. We hurt others. We get sick." We are profoundly social creatures. We may think we want money, power, fame, beauty, eternal youth or a new car, but at the root of most of these desires is a need to belong, to be accepted, to connect with others, to be loved. We pride ourselves on our independence, on pulling ourselves up by our own bootstraps, having a successful career and, above all, not depending on anyone. But, as psychologists from Maslow to Baumeister have repeatedly stressed, the truth of the matter is that a sense of social connection is one of our fundamental human needs. [3]

The most interesting fact about connection is that it has nothing to do with the number of friends you have on

---

[3]https://www.psychologytoday.com/blog/feeling-it/201208/connect-thrive

Facebook or the amount of community groups to which you belong. If you're a loner or an introvert, you can still reap the benefits. How is that possible? A sense of connection is internal. Researchers agree that the benefits of connection are actually linked to your subjective sense of connection. In other words, if you feel connected to others on the inside, you reap the benefits thereof.[4]

    Self-awareness is the key to building the satisfying connections and fulfillment we seek. Until we take the time to understand how we show up in our relationships and are able to clearly articulate our need for love, we will find ourselves repeating defeating patterns of behaviors that sabotage our connections. Our core values drive the qualities we deem important when connecting with others. Our core values are what I deem "the engine of our choices". When we understand the motivation behind our choices, we can make decisions that serve what drives us. Learning the fabric of who you are is fundamental to how you connect with others. We all have innate preferences that are embedded in us from birth. Our innate preferences speak to how we operate. We tend to dismiss necessary connections that offer the fulfillment we seek when we are unable to get past disconnection issues that stem from a lack of understanding preference differences.

---

[4]https://www.psychologytoday.com/blog/feeling-it/201208/connect-thrive

INSPIRED BY LOVE

Awareness is key in these instances. When we are aware of our innate preferences, we can build strategies to create harmony with those who do not share those same preferences. You would be amazed at how many relationships are suffering from merely an innate preference difference. Every day we encounter family members and colleagues who are in relationships and positions that conflict with their core values and innate preferred mode of operation.

As a result, they end up operating in a place of stress instead of strength. There are a variety of personality assessments that provide us with detailed insight into how we are wired, what drives us, how we communicate, how we deal with conflict and stress, and our work and leadership styles. When we have a better understanding of our core make-up, we can begin to align ourselves with what fulfills us and make gratifying connections. As one who analyzes talent for a living, understanding preferences is an integral component in determining job fit. Through my work in HR, I have been exposed to several personality assessment tools that I have found to be beneficial in identifying personality traits and preferences.

One of the ways to begin the work of discovering your personality traits and identifying your innate preferences is by utilizing the Myers Briggs Type Indicator (MBTI). You may take the (MBTI) on-line at *https: www.mbti.online*. The detailed self-report inventory will provide you a comprehensive report with detailed information about your MBTI type profile and references for obtaining more information on how to apply your MBTI type to all areas of your life.

Self-awareness is a gift. Once we are aware of what drives us and how we orient to our world, we can begin to align ourselves with the relationships and professions that provide us the most fulfillment. Self-awareness also provides us indicators of what vocations are better suited for our personality types and which relationships complement our core values. When we enter relationships and professions that are not in alignment with our core values and our places of passion, we become misaligned. We all have the capacity to function outside of our innate preferences and core values.

However, when we find ourselves in consistent misalignment, it breeds discontentment. Consistent frustration and negative emotions are key indicators that we are out of alignment with the strength of who we are. You cannot begin to address your misalignment until you take the time to examine your life and identify what matters to you the most and why. When we are in alignment, we attract experiences and individuals that feed us. We make intentional connections from a posture of understanding what serves us and not haphazardly. Self-awareness gives us the ability to identify what we need to thrive and articulate those needs to others. When we become self-aware, we can begin to communicate our needs and wants in a way that builds intimacy and not resentment. Real intimacy is nakedness of heart. It's what happens when hearts connect without inhibitions and when we see one another in their purest state. Don't overlook divine connections by being hung up on the manner in which it finds you. Love is liberating. Appreciate the gift of having the capacity to give and receive love. It is one of our greatest commodities. You possess a reservoir of treasures that come unlocked when you come into agreement with the grace on your life. You weren't intended to stumble through life underestimating the impact you were intended to make because of your relationship status.

God has faith that you will connect with the creative power that lies within you to become what he purposed for your life. God offered what he loved the most, His only begotten Son, that you would have an abundant life. God trusts the wealth he placed in you to recognize you are enough. The best gift you can offer this world is yourself, your authentic uninhibited fully engaged self, doing what you were born to do. You can offer yourself confidently in liberty when you understand you are fearfully and wonderfully made in an image of a God who masters making masterpieces out of broken vessels.

INSPIRED BY LOVE

Elder Diahann Smith is a teacher, preacher, counselor, mentor and realignment specialist. She is a Human Resources professional with over 25 years of expertise in providing innovative human capital management solutions; recruitment, employee relations management, career development, training and counseling. As Senior Vice President of Human Resources for National Cooperative Bank, (NCB) N.A., Diahann has discovered through her work of identifying and cultivating top talent, the integral relationship between skills and passion when determining individual life purpose. As a certified Myers Briggs Type Indicator (MBTI) practitioner Diahann has been able to leverage the principles of the MBTI tool to educate individuals on the effects of innate preference and passion when seeking life fulfillment. As an Elder under the leadership of Bishop

INSPIRED BY LOVE

Donald Anthony Wright, The Gathering at Forestville, Diahann has been able to utilize her vocational and spiritual training in taking a holistic approach to assisting many in their personal journey of self-discovery. Diahann is a messenger of hope. She is passionate about using the word of God to build, mend and inspire others to apprehend the path uniquely designed just for them. Diahann serves as the Head of the Intercessory Prayer Ministry at The Gathering at Forestville. Diahann holds a Bachelor's degree in Communications from the State University of New York at Fredonia. Diahann is a native New Yorker who currently resides in Waldorf, MD.

LEARNING TO LOVE

Terri Barnes

Typically, as little girls, we often fantasize about what life for us will entail when we grow up. These fantasies are usually extensive and encompass a range of questions regarding our life-long journey. We imagine what our professions will be, the type of car we'll drive, the size and décor of our homes, and the colossal amount of finances our bank accounts will hold.

We imagine the height and build of the man who will sweep us off our feet, the way he'll look at us when he asks for our hand in marriage, the many ways how he'll keep our romance alive and cater to our every need. We don't stop here. The fantasy continues.

We imagine the children we'll have with our husbands, how he'll be present for the births of our God-given miracles and equally excited about each. We fantasize about the attributes our children will share between us and even revisit our decisions as if we actually have a hand in their genetic outcomes.

As little girls, our list of fantasies is endless. Although our thoughts create a visual of the future we hope to have; we fail to take into account the fact that our thoughts are fantasies, merely facets of our imaginations that are perfectly dreamt. However, nothing is ever perfect or happens exactly the way we intend it to; but no one, when we are growing up, tells us this, not even those who love us dearly. This, in effect, was where my issue began... with a fantasy.

INSPIRED BY LOVE

As you may have surmised, I was that little fanciful girl with the perfect dreams. I knew how my life would pan out. I would be in a big house with a fine, rich husband and have everything my heart desired. My profession would be rewarding. Of course, I would be a sought-out singer touring endlessly. Our two children, a boy, and a girl would be perfect. They'd get both my husband's and my undivided attention, want for nothing, attend the finest schools, and would travel with us on tours so that they'd be well-cultured. Ha! I was in for an awakening. Little did I know, then, that fantasizing, as I now know it was naivety and a fatal flaw of mine. It was a fatal flaw because I allowed fantasies to impact my decisions and steer my path of life.

For example, while living life, I searched for that perfect man that I fantasized about so many times before as a little girl. I searched high and low, far and wide, but could not find the man with each of the attributes I'd imagined. When I could not find "the man of my dreams," I settled for those who took an interest in me.

"Mr. Wrongs." These were men who did not "fit the bill;" and, ironically, had not been factored into my many fantasies. Coincidently, each of these men had the same moniker, "Mr. Wrong"; with a distinguishing characteristic that marked the damage they made in my life their numbers. As quick as I mustered the courage to rid of "Mr.

Wrong #1," I met "Mr. Wrong #2;" and, this continued over the course of several years.

Needless to say, I met my share of "Mr. Wrongs," and each made a significant impact in my life, a damaging one. Thus, this "fatal flaw" was one that opened the door to "fatal flaw" number two. Not only had I not considered the number of men I would allow to enter into my life while on my journey to finding "the man of my dreams" (fatal flaw #1). I had not considered the residual effects of the damage they imposed upon me, and the impact these effects would have on my life (fatal flaw #2).

To expound upon these residual effects, no one told me that I would get my heart broken and trampled over – and that it would happen more than once, and that my self-esteem would be shot to smithereens. And, that I would suffer bouts of depression, to name a few of the many ways I suffered at the hand of these men. Needless to say, these episodic moments were cyclical in my life until I realized I had an issue. That is, I didn't love me. Because, I didn't love me; I, secretly, didn't think I deserved to be treated better. So, it was easy to allow a man to "walk over" me.

So often we don't realize that we may be the root cause of what we receive. I believe that our lives are products of our decisions, and mirrors are constant reminders of the products we've become. In other words, mirrors reflect who we really are. As the bible states, ***"You know the tree by its fruit"***[18] *A good tree cannot bear bad fruit, nor can a* *bad tree bear good fruit.[19] Every tree that does not bear good fruit is cut down and thrown into the fire.[20] Therefore, by -their fruits you will know them."* (*Matthew 7:17-20*).

This requires *introspection* – a close look at one's inner self; and, *reflection* – a critique of an outcome. More than once in my life, I have had to take long, hard looks at the patterns in my life. In that time of introspection and reflection, I recognized that I wasn't brave enough to *SEE IT*, *SAY IT* and *SURRENDER TO IT*. What, then, is "*IT*"? Let me explain.

During my times of reflection, I had to *SEE IT* - I had to see that I wasn't happy with me. First, I needed to change my thought patterns. I knew I deserved better in life but was settling for so much less than I'd envisioned. Therefore, I had to believe that God loved me the way HE created me ... that no one thing or person could make me whole or better other than God – and that I was beautiful and worthy enough to be a wife. In essence, each of my "Mr. Wrongs" were not deserving of my attention, and certainly not my love.

During my periods of reflection, I also had to *SAY IT*. *Proverbs 18:21* teaches us that, **"***Death* **and** *life are in the power of the tongue***: and they that love it shall eat the fruit thereof."** Having this belief in God's Word, I had to, actually, say aloud all that I had come to the realization of about me.

INSPIRED BY LOVE

So, dialogue with myself unfolded as such,

"Terri, you aren't happy with your life and what's happening in it; you have to change. Stop allowing men to treat you any kind of way. This means you cannot allow them to only use you for their pleasure. You deserve so much more. Terri, wholeness comes from God alone, and no thing or anyone can fill the void you feel in your heart but God. Terri, you are beautiful and worthy enough to be a "godly" man's wife."

This dialogue served as affirmations from God about me. Because it did, I believed and better accepted God's thoughts about me, which encouraged wise decision-making. Consequently, each time I made decisions, based on these affirmations, I contributed to my life-change. Slowly, but surely, I was "warming up to" a new way of thinking.

To assist in my life-change, there was yet another step that I had to learn to practice; and, it did not come easily. During reflective practices, I began to *SURRENDER TO IT*. This step requires one to consistently practice newly-formed habits. No more "today I will, tomorrow I won't." No more procrastination. No more devising of plans that are obtainable, but never executed – and, certainly, to their degree of specification. This is the point-of-no-return. The point where the "rubber meets the pavement." Needless to say, after one has been accustomed to behaving in a particular manner, and one that is not particularly healthy, all of his or her life, it's hard to change. So, this step is more psychological than verbal. With this said, I had to reprogram my brain by erasing what I had programmed myself to believe, behave, and receive from others. It was time to do what *Romans 12:1-2* teaches us... ***12:1 – "I beseech you therefore, brethren, by the mercies of God, that ye present your bodies a living sacrifice, holy, acceptable unto God, which is your reasonable service." 12:2 – "And be not conformed to this world: but be ye transformed by the renewing of your mind, that ye may prove what is that good, and acceptable, and perfect, will of God."*** Everything about me had to become new again. Therefore, my "new way" of thinking was believing that ***"If anyone is in Christ, he is a new creation; old things have passed away; behold, all things have become new.*** *II Corinthians 5:17.* It was time I not only accepted this fact; but, also actually walked in it.

Learning to Receive Unconditional Love

"There must be a stronger foundation than mere friendship or sexual attraction. Unconditional love, agape love, will not be swayed by time or circumstances".
-- Stephen Kendrick

INSPIRED BY LOVE

We, often, say we desire companionship or a mate to love us beyond measure. Someone who will love us for us; receive us exactly as we are. My question to you as you are reading this book, "When what you have desired and prayed for shows up, will you be able to recognize it; or better yet ,will you receive it?"

Many times, we pray and seek God for this type of love, or relationship and when God answers, we often think we do not deserve it; or, that is too good to be true. We sit back awaiting destruction. We, subconsciously, self-sabotage. Thinking, if we end or destroy it first, we won't risk the chance of being hurt or let down. Well, WRONG!!!!!

When we experience true unconditional, agape love, it does not mean that we won't be hurt or disappointed; but, that love will hold no record of our shortcomings or insecurities. It will not make us feel shame or abuse us; but, will love us through every hurt, insecurity, and shortcoming. Most of all, it will love us and encourage us to be the very best version of who God has created us to become.

The Bible writes about this in *I Corinthians 13,* and I love the Message Bible translation:

Love never gives up.
Love cares more for others than for self.
Love doesn't want what it doesn't have.
Love doesn't strut,

INSPIRED BY LOVE

Doesn't have a swelled head,
Doesn't force itself on others,
Isn't always "me first,"
Doesn't fly off the handle,
Doesn't keep score of the sins of others,
Doesn't revel when others grovel,
Takes pleasure in the flowering of truth,
Puts up with anything,
Trusts God always,
Always looks for the best,
Never looks back,
But keeps going to the end.
Love never dies...

We must first understand the love of God (*I John 4:8*), before we can even attempt to be able to receive the love we so desire from human relationship. We must first learn how to love God, ourselves and then our fellow man. It took me a very long time to understand this concept of relationship. I met a man who began to pour God into me and I had never had that happen before. Someone who saw beyond my physical and sexual appearance and recognized the God in me – it was mind blowing. I, actually, thought he was a bit "off." So, I started to run, not physically, but emotionally. I never had someone to force me to dig deep into my heart, and that was scary and very uncomfortable. I began to resent him and mistreat him, horribly, but the amazing thing is – he never stopped trying nor did he stop loving me. It took me nearly 7 years of tremendous ups and downs to understand unconditional love. His pushing was not about me loving him, but his strong desire for me to love God as much as he did. And, for that, I will always be eternally grateful. He became my husband and through him I learned that God wanted me just as He had created me. I became aware that God loves me, in spite me.

As the scripture states in *Psalm 139:14*: "***I will give thanks and praise to You, for I am fearfully and wonderfully made [...] Wonderful are Your works, And my soul knows it very well.***"

God used my husband to teach me, unconditional love. Unconditional love taught me that I am enough. My world was about to dramatically change and it would my husbands imparted lessons about God's love that served as an anchor during my changing reality. My husband was about to leave me and life was going to require the application of the many truths he permanently etched in my heart.

My world was about to dramatically change and it would be by my husbands imparted lessons about God's love that served as an anchor during my changing reality. My husband was about to leave me and life was going to require the application of the many truths he permanently etched in my heart.

INSPIRED BY LOVE

LESSONS OF LOVE

Losing my husband was probably the hardest thing I've ever had to face. I had just received the gift of having him through covenant as my husband. We were only married a year but our friendship/relationship was for over seven years. He was such a man of wisdom, truly anointed and was a wonderful example of loyalty and God's love. Anthony would often remind me of who I was in God's eyes and talked to me about the many gifts I possessed. His revelations of my gifts were a surprise to me as I was unaware of their existence. If anyone had told me then that this would be the life I would embark upon I would have surely told him or her that they were insane. Losing my husband gave birth to the next phase of my life. It was one of the major steps in becoming a Shepherd of God's people.

Over the years of getting to know Anthony, I didn't realize how much he was imparting into my life. Oftentimes as he shared his wisdom I thought I was just being a good friend and lending a listening ear. Listening to all the ups and downs he faced in ministry, the hurts and betrayals, the victories and triumphs ... all of this was preparing me for the next phase of my life, I just didn't know it. I learned many things from him but here are the biggest four:

INSPIRED BY LOVE

1. GOD USES EVERYTHING

I would often complain about the many things going wrong in my life. I would talk about how I was unhappy with my looks, who didn't like me, who hurt me etc….. Chuck would always say, "*It's working for the good.*" I would get bothered because I didn't understand. I just wanted it to be better or go away. Chuck, as I called him, would remind me of *Romans 8:28*, **"And we know [with great confidence] that God [who is deeply concerned about us] causes all things to work together [as a plan] for good for those who love God, to those who are called according to His plan and purpose."** I had to go through these things in order for me to become the woman God wanted me to become. The good, bad and ugly, God would use it all.

This allows me to be empathetic to anyone who is going through any phase of his or her life. I can assure them that God wastes nothing.

2. ALWAYS LOVE AND HAVE LOYALTY TO PEOPLE

Chuck loved everyone. His big grin, his warmth and spirit would fill any room. If he was for you, he was for you. He was ferociously loyal. I would be amazed at how he would drive for hours to see his big brother coach a

INSPIRED BY LOVE

game or attend a church member's whatever; regardless of how tired he felt after preaching two services on Sunday or leading revival. If Chuck said he was going to be there, he was going to be there...grinning. Watching his dedication to family, church members and colleagues taught me to value and have real relationships.

3. EMBRACE EVERYONE

Embracing everyone was probably the biggest lesson I learned from my husband. We are to meet people where they are and to treat them for who they are becoming and not judge them according to their mistakes. I learned this valuable lesson in our relationship. I made MANY mistakes and Chuck embraced me, continually reminded me of whom I would be and not according to whom I was at that present time. For that I will always be eternally grateful.

4. EXCELLENCE BREEDS EXCELLENCE

Whenever you serve you are to ALWAYS DO SO IN EXCELLENCE. I remember when Chuck became a high school assistant principal. He always wanted to make sure that his principal had everything he needed. He was in a great place of leadership but it didn't stop him from helping the coaches by cutting the grass on the football field, painting the white lines in the parking lot or driving a bus route in his suit and tie to ensure the students were cared for. Whatever He did, He did to the best of his abilities. He would always say, "*excellence breeds excellence.*" I learned the value of serving others by watching him exemplify Christ through service.

There are many other lessons I could share but these four I replay in my mind constantly. Yes, I fall short sometimes but I remember my husband telling me that God uses everything. God has done just that. One of the most difficult times in my life God used it for his glory. I find myself saying often that Chuck and I had to cross paths and through all of our ups and downs it was God working in the both of us to push me and develop me for his glory. I am living out the many truths Chuck's life exemplified about God's unconditional love.

INSPIRED BY LOVE

A native of Jackson, Mississippi, **Pastor Terri D. Barnes** is joyful to serve God's people as a pastor, worship leader and through many other areas of ministry! The journey that the Lord has blessed Terri to walk has been worship-focused from the beginning. A gifted teacher and preacher, Terri also has a beautiful singing voice, which the Lord has powerfully anointed as she continually draws closer to Him in worship. God has anointed this mighty woman with a passionate heart of love for children and a desire to see all people free to worship Christ in Spirit and in Truth. Her expression of ministry in the Body of Christ has evolved from serving as a teacher to a worship leader, which birthed her into the position of Pastor in which she serves today.

On April 22, 2007, Terri joyfully became the wife of Bishop Anthony C. Barnes. Her devotion to serving alongside her husband in ministry was a source of great joy in her life! On June 26th, 2008, the Lord called Bishop

INSPIRED BY LOVE

Barnes home, which God graciously "worked together for good" to help position Terri to answer her calling as shepherd to pastor God's people at Mt. Pleasant Church in Duck Hill, Mississippi. She was ordained on July 31st, 2009, and installed as Pastor of the Mt. Pleasant family the very same day.

The foundation of her ministry is in Lord Jesus' command to pray. Leading by example, Terri knows the power of God to transform a life through the daily "dying to self" required in true prayer. "Jesus replied, 'The hour has come for the Son of Man to be glorified. I tell you the truth, unless a kernel of wheat falls to the ground and dies, it remains only a single seed. But if it dies, it produces many seeds. The man who loves his life will lose it, while the man who hates his life in this world will keep it for eternal life. Whoever serves Me must follow Me; and where I am, my servant also will be. My Father will honor the one who serves me." (John 12:23-26, NIV). With a heart fully committed to serving God and His people, Pastor Terri D. Barnes is truly a powerful and gentle woman after God's own heart.

> *"A trying journey can only result in a phenomenal blessing."*
>
> Dawn M. Harvey

The Wright Kind of Love

Nakia Wright

INSPIRED BY LOVE

I, distinctly, recall a time during a Friday night "Prayer Service" in 2001, when I asked the Lord some very specific questions regarding the desires of my heart. The Lord answered immediately and begun to share with me the answers to those questions. He shared with me, the impact my marriage would have on so many, the happiness my life would hold, and the love my husband would have for me and I for him.

At the time, I was in a relationship that, quite honestly, did not resemble anything close to the view the Lord had shown me, nor did it have even the hope of becoming what He said my relationship would be. This was an extremely pivotal moment in my walk with Christ; from that day until today, I have never forgotten the words He spoke.

*This was my very first introduction to receiving a Word from the Lord. He spoke with me as a friend would. Just as the Lord did to Moses, "**And the Lord spake unto Moses face to face as a man speaketh unto his friend.**" (Exodus 33:11 KJV) He did just that to me.*

This extremely pivotal moment made me trust God in a way I had never done before. In one moment, I learned the biggest lesson, when a word is given for your life you have to trust God with it's timing and walk out the process until full manifestation. When God speaks to us, it is not always for the "here and now." This was my very first encounter with learning to use the power of my wisdom in God. Wisdom is one of the greatest gifts you can possess in your walk with Christ. It is something that I learned through my studies of Solomon that you receive by request to the Lord. Scripture records in I Kings 3:12 (KJV) **"Behold, I have done according to thy words: lo, I have given thee a wise and an understanding heart; so that there was none like thee before thee, neither after thee shall any arise like unto thee."** *Solomon was the only man given an abundance of wisdom, in fact, and he was the wisest man to ever to walk the Earth. Why? Because he asked for it. While I was so intertwined in my right now, the Lord was already in my future. The process of promise will be learned through an ever evolving walk. His words are our motivation. That night in 2001, I asked the Lord something I have shared with very few people. "Lord, let me not miss you." In this moment of intimacy it was if I could ask anything...and I did. The man I am to marry let him be the only man to ever utter this one phrase to me...'I am IN LOVE with you.'*

INSPIRED BY LOVE

God kept his promise. Only one man has ever uttered those words to me! Trust me, I tried to make who I wanted to say, repeat it. Oh how the power of manipulation had a strong hold around my desires. As I sit here thanking the Lord for unanswered prayers, I am living His (my) promise for my life...what joy there is in waiting on God's choice. DRUMROLL PLEASE! It is with a joyful heart – and a promise kept – that I introduce to you, "The Wright Kind of Love." from the heart of Mrs. Nakia Wright.

The Wright Kind of Love

"And the LORD God said, It is not good that the man should be alone; I will make him an help meet for him." Genesis 2:18 (KJV)

What an honor it is to be chosen at such a time as this. Chosen for what you may ask, chosen for greatness! I am honored to be the wife of one of the most influential generals to ever walk the face of this earth Bishop Donald A. Wright. To think God would hand-select the heart of a man once broken; grant him the grace to gather the courage, not to just love again, but trust another being to carry his name, his heart, his dreams, and his destiny. I do not take his choice lightly. In September of 2018, my husband and I will celebrate five years of holy matrimony. Being married has taught me, that the two most powerful words you could ever utter are, "I DO."

Marriage is not a noun, it is a verb.
It is not something you get; It is something you do.
It is the way you love your partner every day.
-Author Unknown

Since the day I became Mrs. Wright, I have felt as if the Lord has bestowed a unique favor upon my life. According to the *Bible*, which is our blueprint of how we are to walk out this life – a man that findeth a wife finds favor with the Lord *(Proverbs 18:22)* and according to his Word when we said, "I Do," the two of us became one. Our oneness granted my husband favor, therefore I became an automatic recipient of the benefits attached to his courage – and my yes. How blessed we are to be walking in the most powerful days of our lives, together. The insight marriage has had on my life has changed the very essence of who I am. We can only hope our living is giving answers to other willing hearts. If you are living and breathing, if you are walking out the promises of God over your life, you **OWE GOD YOUR VOICE**. He trusted you to keep His promise; why should we remain quiet? Knowing what I know now about the power of love, the strength of desire, the excitement of passion, and the boost of motivation marriage has offered me, I feel obligated to share, as often as I can the wisdom of what it truly means, when two become one. It is an honor to have this platform to share the lessons we are learning.

"What you do publicly does not determine the value of your love, it is when no one else is around and you are faced with the singleness of your yes that determines if THIS is your happily ever after."
- Nakia Wright

Join me as we peruse through these next few pages, freely sharing with the world how I see covenant through my eyes. While, I may not have the many years of experience as those reading this book, maybe the freshness of my yes can offer someone to take a new look at their own yes.

INSPIRED BY LOVE

What Does Marriage Mean to Me?

The only advice I can soundly offer – and share – is based on my own personal experience and many days of research. My husband and I have vowed to be relevant answers in the earth. We are not, the **"PERFECT"** couple; does that even exist? Nor do we think we have all of the answers, just because we are Wright's does not mean we are always right. Maybe that was a poor attempt at humor, just wanted to lighten up the mood as we dive into extremely thought-provoking topics. Quite honestly, we are just the opposite. Our sole purpose for freely sharing is simple: Through our imperfections, we have an opportunity to deposit answers in the Earth. When you are ministry minded, you look for places you can deposit the wealth of experience life affords you. If you are considering entering into a covenant of marriage, or you have already stepped into your "I Dos" but find yourself with more questions than answers, or, better yet, perhaps you are the one who is trying to determine if there is a life of happy, "After This", this chapter is for you.

INSPIRED BY LOVE

The man I share life with (my life partner, as I affectionately call him) never asked me to be perfect. I never expected him to be. What we asked for, and promised to each other, was a love that would never fail. Life happens in between so many plans of men. Fluff will not maintain a relationship, nor will it keep a beating heart. The assignment you have as husband and wife is a called place; one you have to be graced to live in and walk out. Rich moments will enhance your marriage. Laughter will keep it alive. Disagreements will occur that will test the very fabric of the strength of your covenant. Tears intentional or unintentional will be shed. Once these moments happen; do you have the appropriate tools to maintain, grow and recover?

We are sending a clarion call to remind the world about the greatness attached to obedience. *DO NOT GIVE UP ON YOUR CALLED PLACE!* **Listen! "Obedience is better than sacrifice."** *1 Samuel 15:22 (NLT)*

I AM LIVING PROOF*! There are benefits attached to being in the will of God that you shall reap in the land of the living.*

INSPIRED BY LOVE

The Wright Kind of Love is an excellent tool (and yes I am biased). Growing up, life did not afford me many opportunities to witness strong examples of the strength of covenant. Through the lenses of my eyes, the reasons a couple got married were simple: It was simply the right thing to do. There was no known purpose attached to two becoming one. Now, knowing what I know, marriage is about fulfilling your God ordained destiny, to fully become who you were called to be in the Earth. The purpose of who you are is deposited in you at birth. Who you are attached to, whether by your own choosing, or through the obedience of the Lord, will determine whether you walk-out the thing you were born to do; or whether you give God a reason to raise up someone else to do what you chose to abort. Who you choose as a life partner will determine which your fate is ultimately. My advice to you….CHOOSE WISELY. Marriage is extremely significant to me. In order to maintain mental balance, I often ask, "Am I a true helpmeet? Can I meet the needs of my husband so that He can become all that God called Him to be in the Earth?" Once I became Mrs. Wright, I have been dedicated to seeing my husband become who God said He would be. Nothing is more important than that to me. His stamp in the Earth is a lamp to the next generation. When I said, "I Do," I agreed to provide the fuel it would take to bring that to pass. ***"For the husband is the head of the wife as Christ is the head of the church, his body, of which he is the Savior."*** *Ephesians 5:23 (KJV)*

Before attaching purpose to marriage, my outlook was limited to having kids, combining two incomes in order to live comfortably, and the pleasures that come along with not living life alone. Based solely on my own personal experiences, if I were asked to summarize what life has taught me about the meaning of marriage, my response would have been, marriage is a weight, the chokehold of life, a source that produces bitterness, anger, frustration, and dead dreams. While this may seem grim, and a little jagged, happiness and marriage TOGETHER was never a point of my reality. Thus, robbing me of any inclination to want it, desire it, or even imagine me in it. The mindset I once possessed could never offer wisdom to the strength of anyone's covenant. This is why it is so very important to evaluate your circle of influence. The ideologies of your circle of influence can be taken on like a bad cold. Choose your circle wisely. The impact your chosen circle has on your life can either be extremely rewarding or profoundly detrimental to your promise. Now that you have been privy to the mind of, *'The Old Me,'* can you imagine the joy I walk in today as a happily married wife? I feel like I broke the curse! I feel as though I am whom I have never seen, none of the credit is of my own. It is truly God all by himself and my desire to want all that He has for me. ***"He created in me a clean heart, renewed in me a right spirit" (Psalms 51:10 KJV).***

Through the Holy Spirit, He is showing me how to be a better wife every day. I have learned happiness is a choice. Happiness does not mean you will not have disagreements, moments of frustration, and times of anger; it simply means these are only moments. The strength of your prayer life, your willingness to forgive, the grace attached to your patience, and the level of your maturity is what ultimately determine the outcome of your marriage.

I carry the assignment of "Wife" proudly and extremely close to my heart. The most appropriate words to express my emotion as Mrs. Wright is simply this:

"And God Remembered Nakia" *(Genesis 8).*

INSPIRED BY LOVE

I want this for you as well. Insert your name after, And God remembered_____. The Lord has no respecter of persons. We can have whatsoever we say, AND whatsoever we work for.

I am learning marriage is what YOU AND YOUR SPOUSE make it. You will often hear me refer to most subjects as, I am still learning; in the words of my husband, I am forever the student. This mindset keeps me balanced. It helps me to always remain mindful. The confidence of who I think I am, would have me thinking of myself higher than I ought to, or like I know it all, or that I have mastered whatever the matter at hand is. The pride attached to this type of mindset would destroy the possibility of growth and halt all possibilities of change in me. Two extremely important factors needed in marriages are growth and change. While the two of you are ever evolving, being slothful and negligent is not an option. We have to be mindful, life will steal vital moments. They can come in the form of parenting, work, church, etc. You have to be intentional about the attention being paid to your spouse. Being present is not enough. Attention has to be paid in the details of love. **#detailsmatter**. Covenant has to be sewn into on a daily basis. Your marriage will mirror the effort you put into it.

> *"Love is intentional, commitment is a choice, and happiness requires work."*
> *- Nakia Wright*

As we just referenced, marriage is a daily work that requires constant attention. What you sow into your union is what you will reap. If you only marry for the benefits and never fulfill the assignment of your union, you run into the fate as many others – failing to bring your union into its fully-intended purpose which leads to an unsatisfied and unfruitful life.

Can you imagine waking up in an unsatisfied world EVERY DAY? The agony it takes to begin a day in discouragement robs you of your strength and your desire to even want to walk the day out. Wow, what a great segway into my next point. We live in an age where everything we want to know is a click away. When you research case studies on why most marriages end in divorce, the common thread is a lack of communication. The path it takes to effectively communicate is a commitment that not many choose to put forth the effort. It truly is the road less traveled. The process to learn how to understand the heart of the one you love, is one that many find as an investment that does not give enough instant gratification. For the sake of this point, I will reference *path.com*. It is one of the more relatable sites with factual data. Path.com studies offer vital information as it pertains to the vibrancy of life versus the lack thereof in a marriage. Path.com's studies have shown that meaningful dialogue is like food for the soul to your spouse. My advice to you will forever be, do not ever stop talking about your dreams, your desires, your failures, and your disappointments with your spouse. Effective communication strengthens the bond of marriage. Commit to the time and the process it takes to not only listen, but to understand, even if you do not agree. My husband and I have to, at times, agree to disagree. It is not confrontational. There are moments the good ole saying that men are from Mars and women are from Venus ring true in the Wright household. Communication is designed to connect two people as one. When you are free to share *LIFE* with your husband/wife you are laying a STRONG foundation, thus ensuring that as each of you grow, you are growing together. Together is key!

INSPIRED BY LOVE

Even in moments, you do not agree; always find space in your heart to be understanding with your spouse. In the words of The Honorable Bishop Donald Wright, "When it comes to a man, he only requires two things – to be respected and to be understood."

As important as it is to freely share through verbal communication, it is just as vital to be an attentive listener. There is nothing more appealing than to have your spouse's undivided attention. A non-distracted moment, breeds a lifetime of benefits. Be intentional in everything you do with your spouse. Their life, their dreams, their promise hinges on it. Communication is one of those things that you will never fully master. As I previously referenced being a student forever is how I approach my marriage. I am always learning. As my husband and I grow, become wiser and add a few more numbers to our age, we change. Change requires readjustment and growth in the both of us. Either way, if we are negligent about the timing of necessary change, it feels as if we are entering moments always in the posture of delay. Delayed timing means the possibility of missing the Lord. Time is the only thing we cannot get back after it is expired. Be sure to be wise stewards over your time, accountable in times that matter the most, and intentional about making your life work. It can be done. It is possible! Some are doing it right now; some are working towards it; .and others are observing it all. Work at love until you become someone's inspiration not to give up.

To my targeted audience, the heart of a wife, I say to you, a wise man once said, "You show me a man that is happy, and I will show you a man destined to be a success." To the wives, I ask you, "Do you have the grace and space in your heart to push a man to the greatest days of his life?"

Leaving All That is Behind
and Walking Into Your Future

"Brethren, I count not myself to have apprehended; but this one thing I do, forgetting those things which are behind, and reaching forth unto those things which are before." *Philippians 3:13 (KJV)*

INSPIRED BY LOVE

I am so very grateful my past did not destroy my future. Let me say that again, in another way – I am so very thankful that my past did not kill the opportunities that lay before me in my present days nor the ones to come!

Our past holds many things. I will speak for myself and say, my past holds great memories, good times, failures, disappointments, blessings, self-induced trauma, pain, suffering, miracles, and restoration. There is an old saying that we have all repeated, time heals all things. However, there has to be an outward manifestation of your choices. I had to walk out the consequences of some of my choices. Time did not simply heal all of them. Some of my choices, God with his sovereign self-came by and did what He does best; just be God. In all areas – either by choice, divine power, or by His grace – I entered into my union with a fresh outlook on life. My memories did not enslave me.

Experience has been one of my premier teachers. The cost attached to my experiences almost cost me my right mind. This is why I attempt to convey to my children, that I have been through enough storms and traveled down enough paths in life that you should never, willingly, choose to go down some roads. Take heed to my lessons and do not allow experiences to be your principal teacher in life.

INSPIRED BY LOVE

Wisdom will save you years of turmoil. Wisdom by far is a much GREATER teacher. It is life's life jacket. It will keep you from drowning in the sea of life.

Without a desire to want to live a fulfilling life, the four inches of space between your ears will destroy you and all who enter your path – if you allow it. Given the power and opportunity, a memory can become a tsunami to your life. You will decay from the inside out. If you have given too much time and attention to the memories of your past, I admonish you, in this very hour, to break the stronghold it has had on you. Turn off the thing called "your memory." Memory will remind you of who you were, but it does not have the capability to show you who you will become. Stop giving your past all of who you are. As my husband often shares, operate in the manner your body was designed to function. Your eyes are in the front of your head, and they are designed for you to see what is ahead of you. Your mouth is on the front of your face; it is designed for you to speak those things that are before you. Everything vital to your being faces the direction in which you are headed, and that is forward. So why do we spend so much time on what's behind us?

INSPIRED BY LOVE

How do I cut off my memory? So glad you asked. During an extremely vulnerable time in my life I recall praying a prayer that saved my life, *"Lord until you remove the memory, I ask as humbly and as sincerely as I know, remove the sting attached to the thought. I thank you for it in advance, right now, in Jesus' name."* I can recall praying this prayer like it was yesterday. I believe the Lord allows this to be embedded into my memory for a day such as this, for the moment to be someone's answer. I share with you what saved me from me. Believe God for the freedom from the bondage of your own thoughts! All we have to do is give God a reason. He is MORE THAN ABLE!

Turn your thoughts to the things that turn on the creative side of your being. The moment your past begins to enter into your thoughts, intentionally focus on your promise and begin to build it. Do it until the only thoughts consuming your mind is your future.

> *"History is your yesterday. Faith is your tomorrow. Focus on your faith."*
> **Bishop Donald Wright.**

INSPIRED BY LOVE

And the Conversation Continues

"Trust in the Lord with all your heart and lean not on your own understanding; in all your ways submit to him, and he will make your paths straight." *Proverbs 3:5-6 (KJV)*

One of the many ways to be swept off of your feet is through meaningful and intentional moments. When a couple shares, "I am married to my best friend;" I inquire what produces this type of bonding. Nine out of ten times, I have heard, "Because we talk about everything and we do the things we enjoy, together." Sharing your life with your partner secures a STRONG foundation for happiness to be built on.

Let's be clear, I am not the one who will talk about the enemy much, neither will I give him much attention in this chapter – he is already defeated. I do, however, believe in the inerrancy of Scripture, and it is recorded in *James 4:7,* **"Submit yourselves therefore to God. Resist the devil, and he will flee from you."** I truly believe my inner me is my greatest undefeated enemy. However, there is a very real devil. In my life, I function from an ownership position.

According to the Bible, the enemy has absolutely no power over me. With this being said, depending on your mate's level of maturity, be as open as your spouse is able to handle your past. This openness does many things. It frees you from feeling as if you are hiding parts of your life and you eliminate living in fear, praying that a part of your life does not meet you head on. Do not give the enemy power to dangle shame or embarrassment of your past choices over you. FREE YOURSELF! Be open and honest. If you can recall how we opened this chapter, perfection does not exists.

Your choices, whether they are the ones you are proud of or not, are what made you who you are. When you embrace who you are, the shame that we have all felt in life begin to drop off. Embrace **YOUR AFTER YOUR, LIFE HAPPENS**. There is nothing you should torture yourself over, nor anything you allow the enemy to taunt you with in your thoughts, for they can lead to hidden shame and guilt. *There can never be a full becoming of self with potential hidden dangers from your yesterdays.* I thank God for the foundation of strength that was laid on the table prior to my marriage. My husband and I got it all out. Not all at one time, of course, but with consistent open and unending conversations; better yet said, "We continued the conversation again, again and again."

Communication, "Yes", we have returned to this topic. Do not ever stop talking to your spouse. When you are free, open, forgiving, and understanding, you establish a safe-haven that will breed sharing and truth. Do not keep score. If you are unintentionally wounded in the sharing process, respond in truth, not rage. Rage will cause your spouse to shut down and become apprehensive about what is acceptable versus unacceptable to share.

Anger and resentment builds barriers. Whatever you do, strive not to have barriers around your heart. The full purpose of your union can never be birthed in this environment. Reminder - sharing frees you of your past and propels you into a glorious and promising destiny of holy matrimony. Be intentional in your letting go and be precise in your embrace of promise. Your future looks bright. It looks free. It is worth it. How much are you willing to put into making it come to pass?

INSPIRED BY LOVE

Tips on How to Begin the Conversation

1. Share with your spouse one or two reasons you fell in love with them. In return ask what that was one defining moment when they knew you were the one.
2. Inquire of your spouse; tell me something I do not know about you.
3. Share with your spouse a defining moment in your life that either made you desire to love them more or made you love them through a slight hesitation. In return, ask the same of them.

**Note: When you are preparing to be vulnerable and open, be mindful of your tone and approach. This diffuses the apprehension of sharing and does not feel like an interrogation.

Keep in mind, never ask a question you may not be strong enough to handle the answer. Truth sometimes can be painful. If you are not strong enough for truth, **NEVER** enter into a dialogue out of curiosity **ONLY**. If your ultimate goal is not to love and know your spouse better, do not enter into any discussions.

Aim to be your spouse's best friend. For many of us we know we can live alone, the true barometer of a relationship for me, is how well can live together? Can we do so with happiness and peace? Does our level of forgiveness, grace, and mercy stretch enough to even be a product of a happily ever after? A marriage is stripped of its power when you tolerate one another and don't freely love. Your marriage will never look similar to anyone else's. Opinions can be a cancer to a marriage. Work not to solicit the opinion of others. Unless their words are tested and proven, guard spousal moments with everything you have: your life, your hope, your future; your promise depends on it. Honor your union! There is an unspoken code in any relationship that should always be adhered to, love covers. Never uncover the one you love. Especially in the moments where your emotions are at their highest!

What Happens When I Enter Into Covenant and It Looks Nothing Like What I Envisioned?

You cannot give up on someone because the situation is not ideal. Great relationships are not great because problems are non-existent, they are great because both

INSPIRED BY LOVE

people care enough about the other person to find a way to make it work.

- Author Unknown

The Strength of What Marriage Truly Is

Your measure of love and "stick-to-itiveness" will depend, highly, on your willingness to forgive AND forget. How many times have we heard, "I forgive my husband or my wife, but I will not ever forget the wrong they did to me?" You have just chosen to keep "a moment" prisoner in your mind. You just gave yourself the option to hoard it as ammunition for a future time of need. I ask, for the sake of giving you space to make a mental note to reference later, why?

Please Note: For those spouses who are in an emotionally or physically, abusive relationship, I suggest you seek immediate attention from a trusted source. Neither form of abuse should ever be tolerated in a loving unit of holy matrimony. YOU ARE WORTH MORE THAN THAT. YOUR LIFE MATTERS TOO MUCH TO LIVE IN THAT TYPE OF ENVIRONMENT.

INSPIRED BY LOVE

In your marriage vows, you promised one another until death do us part. If it is a lifetime commitment you are after, why would you intentionally abort the opportunity of happiness in your life? Many view marriage as a fairy tale. As a young lady in my early 40's, with their being seemingly a shortage of African-American Christian men, we have all heard our girlfriends say, "I cannot wait to get married. I look forward to the day when I go to sleep and wake up to my husband." Or, "I am tired of eating alone. I cannot wait until God sends me my husband, so I can go home and eat dinner with him. And, "BILLS, I cannot wait until the day when someone comes along to take care of me." Wait, my favorite of them all, "do not let the winter season come upon me alone, the ladies cringe at the thought of getting snowed in without a snuggle partner. The surface benefits and thoughts of marriage are what many of us look forward to. We do not think of the times when life breaks our partner, and it is our prayers and love that have to be strong enough to make him or her whole again. Nor do we give thought to the timeframe between actuality and manifestation when your spouse is working/building who they will ultimately become. What happens when our spouse hurts or disappoints you? These are the very moments that our love and the very fabric of what God created our unions to be is being tested.

Each of us have a power that supersedes the power of prayer, and it's called *our will*. You can pray for a situation until the sun rises and falls, but if you choose not to forgive and understand, the matter will linger and become almost like cancer to your covenant. Do not allow unforgiveness and stubbornness to drive your relationship to unimaginable places.

Just for the sake of help, let me share a proven fact, God's response to us are synonymous with that of "a perfect of a gentleman". He will not go in any unwelcomed places. If you block Him from certain mental spaces in your marriage, He will not force himself there. You have to, willingly seek His power and plan in painful places in order for Him to have full control over your life and union. No one in their own power can make a Godly union successful.

HAPPINESS IS A CHOICE and I REPEAT HAPPINESS IS A CHOICE! When making necessary choices with your life, remove your emotions from the equation. Emotions can be misleading and many times are very temporary. Making permanent decisions at the height of an emotional moment has the power to bring something called an exit strategy into your relationship. If there is no threat of emotional or physical abuse, there should be no exit strategy. After all, you took a vow and in that vow did you give yourself an "OUT" option?

Please Note: I am a product of divorce. I know life happens. However, I am addressing an audience who have chosen to fight for their marriage, those who have chosen to find happiness at any cost and to those who want better but have no idea of how to obtain it. For the sake of building the Kingdom, saving your family, or walking out your dreams, choose to be a wife or husband for life. As simple as it sounds, make that your motto; "I am a wife or husband for life." Your words have power. Speak life over your promise!

Engaged: Enter into your union with a clear mind, vowing to commit all of who you are to your spouse. Do not enter with an exit strategy. If you are even entertaining that thought, you should seriously reconsider whether marriage is the right choice for your life.

Married: Find a clear mind and vow to commit all of who you are to your spouse. Take all exit strategies off the table. Seek counseling if necessary. Often times the voice of an experienced individual can help you understand one another. Not everyone is an effective communicator, this has to be learned, if there is no teacher to do the instructor present you may need to seek assistance. Marriage is worth fighting for. This is truly by any means necessary type of vow to keep. FIGHT FOR YOUR MARRIAGE! The *Bible* says, ***"It is not good for man to be alone."*** If God's original plan was a forever kind of love, why would we abort His will?

Our Family Dynamic

What is the definition of the term, "Blended Family"?

Urban Dictionary: Anyone, after their latest marriage, that looks at their children and realizes they have half-siblings, a biological sibling, and step-siblings.

Webster's Dictionary: A family that includes children from a previous marriage of one spouse or both.

LovetoKnow.com: A "blended family" is one where the parents have children from previous relationships, but all the members come together as one unit.

The Wright's Family Definition: When we all come together under one roof, we are just one big family, simply "family". In today's society, the word "blended," Nakia's opinion is about to be inserted here, has the potential to steal the power out of one big happy family. I entered into marriage with two children. From the moment I said, "I do," my husband spoke of Kayla and Semaj as if they were his seed. In his mind, that is just what he believed. I adored him so much for this manner of love. Placing a "title" on a relationship frames your mindset of how you, consciously and subconsciously handle it. Case in point, if my husband adopted the philosophy of a "blended" family, in his mind, he could, subconsciously, treat Kayla and Semaj as if he was raising someone else's children. Whether knowingly or unknowingly, you place barriers of how far you are willing to go. Why? Because these are not your children. The authentic flow of love that is formed towards the children you birth is unmatched. As much as you say you love another child, the love you have for your own, cannot be compared. Please do not inappropriately title your family dynamic. I thank God for the wisdom, heart, and understanding of my husband; he teaches me often true love is pure.

How do you make this new merge of lives work? Be open! Sugar-coated conversations are never productive.

Our children today understand more at their young ages than what we did. It is the nature of our society. The *Bible* says, **"Train up a child in the way that he or she should go."** You cannot accurately train, lead, and create greatness behind a cloud of dishonesty.

The only advice I can offer is what worked for The Wright's. It is my hope the truths of our dynamic would one day save someone else's life. When children are involved, always make them feel a part of the merging of families. Share with them your heart and be sure to show them where they fit in the equation. I chose to be very detailed in explaining the change that was about to take place in our lives. I recognized after I said I do, everything they once knew would suddenly change. Since my children are visual, I drew a heart and in it were sections; one section had God, the other family and friends, another Kayla and Semaj, and, lastly, my husband. In each of these sections, I clearly explained only those identified in the labeled sections could produce love for that area. There was no way Kayla or Semaj could fulfill the space in my heart occupied in the husband area and vice versa; in the God area, no matter how much my children loved me and I them, that love would never be enough to fulfill the God area. I further explained how impossible this was physically and emotionally. I also had to make it known that the love in the area where their names were could never be overshadowed, overrode, nor replaced by any other section of my heart. Thankfully, it was well-received. They both wanted to see me happy. Most children desire to see their parents happy. How you ultimately handle this is based on your relationship with your child. I simply wanted to offer an example to begin a conversation or at least, open your mind on where to start. Happiness does not just happen. It requires work, it demands difficult moments, it involves understanding; and, most importantly, it requires that you show up at every moment. Again, make healthy dialogue a part of your daily routine. A vital lesson life has taught me is, imperfect days create learning lessons. Anything worth having takes work, forgiveness, laughter, and patience. Command YOU to always summons strength to fight for your family, give YOU NO OPTIONS!

Where Do We Go From Here

Marriage is a powerful union. It is one that can make a man do one of two things: produce the greatest him he has ever seen, or break him until he forgets the power he was born to possess.

My favorite books that clearly define the complete understanding of a man and how he goes after the things he was born to do are: **"Tonight We Wrestle" by Dr. Donald A. Wright** *(Yes that is my husband. Feels like a shameless plug; but it is the truth!) and,* **"Wild at Heart" by John Eldredge.**

My previous statement is an accurate truth for women too. Marriage can either give her a chance in life that far exceeds her expectations; or make her feel as if she is living a life of torment, bondage, and broken dreams.

The most impactful books I have read, as it pertains to the picture of a woman, are: **"Discovering the Mind of a Woman" by Ken Nair** *and,* **"If Only He Knew" by Gary Smalley.**

Lend me your imagination for a moment, as I attempt to express the impact you have on the future of your spouse. As an individual who works in the Christian community and in a world heavily influenced by social media, expressing your feelings publicly have become a growing trend. I am led to believe, many enter marriages without realizing the totality it is designed to possess. In a day where commitment seems to be the unpopular choice, when a man chooses to give his name to a woman he is making a HUGE statement. In most cases, he is saying, "I cannot make it without you. I have become all of who I can become alone, and now I need a helpmeet to walk out my assignment as a whole man."

It is a biblical principle, *Proverbs 18:22 (NIV)* **states, "He who finds a wife finds what is good and receives favor from the Lord."** It is not good for man to be alone. Do you know the keys of destiny that are unlocked when you find favor with the Lord through holy matrimony? Hold the destiny of your mate in your heart as if his/her life depends on it. In all sense of truth, it does. Keep it well-groomed and cared for. Be sure not to allow your love to mirror a dried up desert. Water your love, keep God first, preserve your promise...your efforts are their lifeline.

Keep Your Love Fresh and Let It Always Be Sweet

My husband and I have been married for four years. Many will say we are still newlyweds. I would agree. It is my heart's desire to always treat my marriage as if we are lifelong newlyweds. My mindset is that our love will not ever grow stale. For all intent and purposes, I will repeat what I have heard my husband say time and time again, to the couple whose been married for 25 years you, too, are newlyweds. The person you married 25 years ago and the person you are married to now, is not the same person. If you are still loving, expecting, and communicating with your spouse the same as you did 25 years ago, I will venture out on a limb to say there is a deficiency in your union. Growth happens, change is inevitable, with or without your participation – it happens. If you are not a part of the process, nine times out of ten, you will follow down the path of the, "We have grown apart couples." Be intentional in your commitment to your covenant. Ask your spouse daily about their day. If they say, "I experienced a good day," inquire about what that means. If their response is, "I had a bad day;" again, I admonish you to inquire about the difficulties of their day; and, without being prompted, end the conversation in prayer. Thank God openly that your spouse survived a trying day, decreeing and declaring that not only will their tomorrow be GOOD, but they can always find strength in your arms. Openly pray for your spouse. Not only does that show your love for them in the natural, it also speaks to the intensity of your love for them spiritually. There is a certain kind of assurance that solidifies their tomorrow, knowing it's already covered. What spouse would not run home to that every day? You have just covered them in two worlds.

Paying attention is extremely vital! We have so many opportunities to deposit seeds of strength, happiness, and a lot of "I got you's" if we are in tune with his/her needs. Try as hard as you can to always be attentive to the needs of your spouse. Your union requires your undivided attention to be a success!

The Conclusion of the Matter

A Note Taken from Pathos.com
"Every good and loving relationship requires a degree of patience. We hope that by allowing someone time to grow, and the grace to do so, we will eventually receive our reward for waiting. The difference in a relationship with God in the midst is that your patience is always rewarded. It may not have fit your schedule, and it may not look the way you thought it would, but it will come exactly when it was supposed to. Give God a chance to do His work and

allow Him to do it on His schedule. He will make everything work out just right, just as He sees fit, and He will do it right on time."

***A WRIGHT NOTE:** Never allow an outside influence to determine what your marriage should and should not resemble. **YOU DEFINE THE PARAMETERS OF YOUR "I DO"** and watch God cause your union to bud, bloom, and blossom into something beautiful to behold!*

Holy Matrimony is powerful, but the question has to be asked – would it be so hard for you to choose to abandon stale, failed memories of the past and opt out for a better future? You do have the ability to break the power over past emotions! You do have the mental fortitude not to choose to allow past failures, past pleasures, past disappointments and life's uncertainties to hold you in psychological bondage. Sound an alarm to yourself!

Your new life awaits you. It is calling you so loudly into a place of peace, happiness and better days. Answer the call and ENJOY your life. Live your life, do not merely exist!

As we conclude the sentiments of my heart, I speak a

fresh anointing over your marriages. I speak life in you to want to run on and see what the end shall be, and I stand with you as you look forward to walking out the very BEST days of your life. **#therearenotesfromnakia** - The Wright Kind of Love will NEVER look similar to your marriage. You create your own marriage and make it work. This is the framework of my life. I share with you in hopes to be a relevant answer in the Earth – leaving a loud legacy for others to follow.

Until we meet again....

INSPIRED BY LOVE

Dr. Nakia Renee Wright is a woman who wears many hats. She is a wife, mother, counselor, mentor, and motivational speaker, among many other things. However, first and foremost Dr. Wright is a servant to her Lord and Savior, Jesus Christ and believes, without wavering, in the strength of Holy Writ.

Dr. Wright has fulfilled many accomplishments in her career and ministry. She currently serves as the Chief Operating Officer for The Gathering at Forestville, serving under the leadership of Bishop Donald A. Wright. In 2010 Dr. Wright started The Chosen Ones, a ministry geared towards young women ages 13 – 17 in an effort to combat the daily struggles that teenage girls face. She seeks to uplift, strengthen, and speak life into these young women by being a transparent vessel that is dedicated to the success of every heart she encounters.

Dr. Wright has been an advocate for the advancement of services for the disenfranchised all her life. In 2013 Dr. Wright's exemplary and ongoing community service was recognized and she received her Doctorate in Philosophy.

In March she was among seven great women appointed to the leadership team of the Global United Fellowship's Pastors Wives Division, where Bishop Neil C. Ellis is the Presiding Prelate. In April of 2016, Dr. Nakia Wright hosted her very first women's symposium entitled, Repowering Your Strength. It was from this symposium that A Woman's Voice (AWV) was birthed. Today, A Woman's Voice is a nonprofit organization birthed to recognize the need in the Earth for women of all different walks of life to come together to be repowered, encouraged, educated, uplifted, inspired, and renewed. Dr.

INSPIRED BY LOVE

Nakia Wright leads several initiatives encompassing AWV's mission.

The Life of Books a nationally online syndicated monthly book club on WLS Radio (Listenvisionlive.com) which promotes the importance of reading by sharing Dr. Nakia Wright's and her panel's insight on their selected book of the month. Dr. Nakia also hosts her own monthly radio show where she uses her platform to spotlight causes, organizations, and events that support women empowerment and building strong relationships within families and marriages.

Dr. Nakia Wright is married to The Honorable Bishop Donald A. Wright, the two currently reside in Bowie, Maryland with their children and granddaughter.

Overcoming the Stronghold of Depression

Regina Randolph-Davis, MSW

INSPIRED BY LOVE

You Can Overcome Anything! And I Can Show You How

As a practicing, licensed Psychotherapist for many years, I have encountered so many people who have issues plaguing them that keep them from achieving all they can in life. Many spend their lives trying to find solutions to their problems but are never able to completely solve them, so they never succeed in life – beyond what they can handle with these, seemingly, unresolvable problems. But on the flip side, as a born-again believer, I have seen the most difficult problems solved by the power of God so often, that I am convinced there is only one true source that we can tap into to solve any problem – the life-changing gospel of Jesus Christ! Many people discount this; particularly, those with humanistic thinking. But, I want to share some overwhelmingly convincing evidence with you concerning the only way I have discovered to completely overcome anything! *"For with God nothing will be impossible" Luke 1:37*

Psychology is the study of behavior and mind. The world knows, and has ways of trying, to help you through scientific means; but, they have yet to discover how to totally heal your mind. Yes, they have medications that help, but with the exception of a few minor psychological disorders, they have no cure for the most common mental health disorders that keep people from functioning at their full potential. This leaves a significant portion of our population in a less than optimal situation. Unfortunately, this number includes a lot of people who are believing God for the healing of their mental and emotional health issues.

In my book *How to Overcome Anything: Tools for Living a Victorious Life*, I write about how many common disorders and mental health issues keep people from living the lives God intended for them. I discuss several common disorders that I have discovered to be the most prevalent in my experience.

In my practice, for many years my favourite type of therapy was, and still is, solution focused. *Solution Focused Therapy* (SFT), as its name suggests, focuses on solutions and is goal-oriented, rather than problem focused as many other therapies are. My goal is to show you the pathway, or solution, to freedom from these issues and lay a pattern that you can use to Overcome Anything!

Depression, Grief and Chronic Sadness

Weeping may endure for a night, but joy comes in the morning! It really does!

How do I know? I've had personal experience and personal encounters with so many people who have experienced all three of these issues. This is the most common disorder I have seen in all of my years of practice.

85 percent of the patients I have seen have a diagnosis of depression. Keep in mind that depression has many causes, and not all of them show up in the literature we have about depression. Although depression does not discriminate and I have seen my share of depressed men, most of the people I have helped with depression have been women. Men are less likely to seek help for depression. Instead, they may self-medicate with alcohol, drugs, or a more permanent solution-suicide.

Major depression involves a number of symptoms, including feeling chronically sad, hopeless, worthless, and helpless, losing interest in things that used to be pleasurable, lack of energy, difficulty concentrating and remembering, sleep problems, appetite changes and restlessness, irritability, and suicidal thoughts. This kind of depression can happen once in a person's life, or it can be chronic. It is usually severe and persists for at least two weeks, causing interference in daily living activities. In some cases, the depression may include suicidal thoughts or behaviors and/or even psychotic symptoms in which the person is out of touch with reality and not thinking clearly.

Some common causes of depression are:
- Loss of relationships, circumstances, situations, expectations, and dreams.
- Significant life transitions, a major move, divorce, mid-life crisis, empty nest.

- Chronic medical conditions
- Physical changes in the body, stroke, heart attack, cancer, hormonal or thyroid disorders,
- Personality traits such as perfectionism, pessimism and being overly dependent -Stressful changes in life patterns
- Unresolved anger
- Unrepentant sin and disobedience
- Occult involvement- I discuss this in chapter two of my book
- Negative thinking patterns, at the core of depression
- Multiple stressors or feeling overwhelmed by stress
- Side effects of medications, high blood pressure, steroids and others
- Alcohol and drug intoxication and withdrawal
- Diet, specifically, low levels of folic acid and vitamin B12
- Degenerative neurological conditions such as Alzheimer's and Huntington's disease
- Viral infections, such as hepatitis and mononucleosis

The enemy would love nothing more than to wear us

out and wear us down so that we will have no power to overcome life's challenges. If he can't kill us, he can render us helpless and hopeless so that we will be ineffective when it comes to living out God's plans for our lives. Some walk around saying, "Well, I guess that's the way things are now, and there is nothing I can do about that. I can't change anything; it's useless and hopeless. I can't do anything worth anything; I'm worthless and useless." If he can get us to think like this, he has done a pretty good job of rendering us useless for the kingdom and our families.

"And he shall speak words against the Most High God and shall wear out the saints of the Most High and think to change the time and the law…" Daniel 7:25

For some, depression is actually a welcomed feeling, as it can be addictive, a safe hiding place. They long to nurse their wounds because it feels good to withdraw and isolate from everything around them.

There is hope, however, for people who are experiencing depression.

This is God's therapeutic plan to overcome depression, sadness, and grief. It's the best Solution Focused Therapy (SFT) ever, in my opinion! It's found in *Isaiah 61:3*:

"To console those who mourn in Zion, to give them Beauty for ashes, the oil of joy for mourning, the garment of praise for the spirit of heaviness

That they may be called trees of righteousness, the planting of the Lord, that He may be glorified."

While the enemy wants to wear us out, God wants to refresh us. Every time we are sad or depressed, God wants to give us joy and happiness. He's not saying go into your past and deal with the things that caused the depression; on the contrary, He keeps us in the present and gives us the solution. God is the Master Psychologist!!

He also tells us in *Isaiah 60:1 (AMP):*

"Arise from the depression and prostration in which circumstances have kept you rise to a new life. Shine for the glory of the Lord is upon you!"

This is therapy at its best! The goal in any therapy session is to tell you that you can be successful, you can overcome the circumstances that have you physically and mentally stagnant, and that you can rise above your circumstances and have a better outlook on life. This is directly from God.

Sadness, which is a normal reaction to loss or painful circumstances, should lessen and become easier to deal with over time. Your emotional makeup is such that you should feel sad when something goes wrong, someone gets hurt, a loved one dies, you break up with your girlfriend, your friend moves away or other issues involving loss occur. This sadness might not ever disappear, but it isn't crippling. However, if you find yourself stuck in that sad feeling and unable to move on with life, you might be depressed, stuck in sadness or grief.

Grief is our response to a significant loss, particularly the permanent loss of someone or something to which we have a bond or connection, such as the death of a loved one, a divorce, or some unexpected tragedy.

"Normal" grief goes away with time and almost always presents itself in stages. The five stages of grief are: denial and isolation, anger, bargaining, depression, acceptance. It's possible, however, to get stuck in a stage of grief for extended periods of time. This is called "Complicated" grief. Some get stuck in the Depression stage. When this happens, grief therapy / counseling becomes necessary. Grief and sadness are meant to be temporary. However, depression can linger for months or years and can become chronic, recurring throughout your life.

Depression affects the body, mood, thoughts, and soul. It is more than normal sadness or feeling down. It's a persistent sadness that permeates most aspects of your life: sleeping, eating, working, communing with God, socializing and enjoying life.

Depression is serious and debilitating, not something you just snap out of overnight. And, it is not just "all in your head." That's why, if you are just sad or "down in the dumps," you should not say that you're depressed. You are not depressed; you are sad. Trust me, these terms are not synonymous, and you would rather be sad than depressed.

The most common cause of depression is – negative thinking. Sure, at the point of depression there is a chemical imbalance. More than likely, you are not producing serotonin (or "feel good") chemicals in the amounts necessary to balance your mood. But, does the chemical imbalance cause the negative thinking; or, does the negative thinking cause the chemical imbalance?

Although we don't know which happens first, it is known that if you can change a person's thinking, you can change their chemistry and cure the depression.

Romans 12:1 says: **"Be not conformed to this world but be transformed by the renewing of your mind."**

Negative thinking leads to negative emotions, which leads to negative perceptions, which reinforce negative thinking. It's a cycle. It produces hopelessness in both your actions and your thoughts. For example, you have thoughts like "That person does not like me;" "That can never happen for me;" "I will always be in this situation;" "I'm not good enough; my situation is hopeless, and I am helpless to do anything about it;" "This kind of thing always happens to me, it's only going to get worse;" and, "He / she doesn't love me."

Negative thinking is behind most depression. It

almost always gives you a negative view of yourself, the world and the future. In order to combat depression, we have got to break past the lies associated with it to be free.

There is even a lie that Christians should never get depressed. We are human, we become sad and we grieve too! It's just a lie the enemy uses to keep our depression hidden so we will suffer in silence and never get free. There are many causes of depression. Some are directly related to spiritual issues, but others are not.

Many people in the *Bible* experienced depression: Hanna, David, Elijah and Naomi are just a few of them. In the book of Ruth, Naomi was so depressed she didn't even want to acknowledge who she was anymore; she wanted to do away with herself and become someone else, thinking all was lost and her situation was hopeless. She became very negative about her situation. She even changed her name from Naomi, which means "pleasant," to Mara, which means "bitter." Naomi was stuck in a deep depression.

God wants us to have a pleasant life, but the enemy wants us to be bitter about life and not understand the "big picture" and, that our lives were meant to be lived with joy.

God's word tells us that there is a cure for depression. **"God is not like man, that he should lie."** *Numbers 23:19.* He tells us there will be sometimes of sadness, grief, and depression, but lets us know *"that weeping may endure for* *a night (a season), but joy comes in the morning!"* Your situation is not hopeless!

Sin can sometimes be the root of depression. It can stem from getting involved in things and relationships that are not good for us; but, more often than not, negative thinking is the main culprit. Negative thinking develops out of life experiences. People who suffer sexual abuse, grow up in the homes of alcoholics or drug abusers, live through messy divorces, lose a loved one to death, cope with chronic illness or experience financial problems often experience trauma, abuse, abandonment or neglect. These experiences make us vulnerable to the lies of the enemy.

Ungodly soul ties can cause depression because they almost always involve some type of abuse – either emotional, physical, sexual. A vicious cycle ensues of breaking up and making up that lays a destructive pattern on your soul for depression to occur over and over again, laying emotional tracks so that even when you finally end the relationship. Those patterns of depression remain in your soul, longing to resume the familiar cycle. You can be in a good marriage and you wonder why you are experiencing depression. It's that familiar cycle that resurfaces in your life as you deal with normal challenges. It tries to make you relive the emotions you felt during those years of ungodly soul ties. Your entire soul is affected (mind, will and emotions). You have to give attention to each area of your soul in order to totally get rid of the depression. Your mind – renewed; your will – restored; and, your emotions – healed.

The enemy tries to discourage us and convince us that life is hopeless. Our minds are fertile ground for attack when our defenses are down. Because we hurt, we give him access. When depression hits, your relationship with God becomes depressed, too. You feel disconnected. God seems far away and aloof. You believe He is unable or doesn't want to help you, then you feel totally discouraged. A lot of depression is situational. That means depression comes as a result of what your situation is, what happens to you, or what happens around you.

It's a response to life's losses and hardships. Usually they are big losses, like a parent diagnosed with a terminal illness, losing your spouse to death or divorce, family trauma like a child with severe health challenges, losing your home to foreclosure or some life-altering event, like becoming a single parent and being unable to care for your children properly, or a lost love relationship. It can be that you become depressed in your marriage because you are not receiving love the way you need to. Your level of contentment is based on whether your situation or circumstance is good or bad. I have seen a lot of women who have been married for several years become depressed due to the state of their marriage. They have to take antidepressants and come to talk therapy. One woman told me that her husband killed all of the love on the inside of her.

After the birth of a child, postpartum depression may or may not be due to hormone fluctuations, but due to a life change circumstance. Moving to a new city, town or state. This is called Adjustment Disorder and may cause depression, as well.

Depression can result from not being able to deal well with people, circumstances, and expectations. We can, actually, bring on depression by the way we think and respond. Our response to situations can determine if we will become depressed. It is very important that we understand what depression is and how we can overcome this condition.

Depression is a mood disorder which impacts more than 350 million Americans. It's the Leading cause of disability in this country, and it appears to affect more women than men. Serious depression debilitates the individual and can tear apart families. However, depression is treatable. Unfortunately, most people who have depression don't get help. Life can become very difficult and not worth waking up for in the morning. But there is good news, you can overcome depression!

INSPIRED BY LOVE

How to Overcome Depression

Ask yourself, "Am I really depressed; or, am I sad or grieving?" Identify the depression and acknowledge it. *Prov. 12:25, **"Anxiety in the heart of man causes depression. But a good word makes it glad."***

Take a long walk in the park several times a week. Soak in sunlight as you walk. Getting enough Vitamin D is important.

Ask God for help and trust Him. *Psalm 121:1-2 (MSG)*: ***"I look to the hill where my help comes from, my help comes from the Lord."***

"Praise Him despite the circumstances." *Phil. 4:1.*

"Be anxious for nothing but in all things give thanks."

CBT: ***"Change your negative thoughts and replace them with the Word of God."***

Romans 12:2: ***"Be not conformed to this world but be transformed by the renewing of your mind."***

"Meditate on the Word of God." *Joshua 1:8*

"Assess how you are feeling every morning and give thanks!" *Psalm 5:3*

Exercise 30 minutes per day for at least 5 days per week and choose a healthy diet. Make yourself do it. Don't wait to feel it. Make plans to change your environment even for an hour per day go to a beautiful park or do something you really like doing. *Proverbs 17:22:* ***"A merry heart is like medicine."***

Ask yourself, "What caused your depression?" Anger, conflicts with family members, guilt for something you feel responsible for. ***"Forgive yourself and others."*** Acts 24:16

Get evaluated for medication if you are still feeling depressed after doing the above for 2-3 weeks. Serotonin levels may need a jump. If you take an anti-biotic for an infection, you can take an anti-depressant for depression. It can help.

God does not want you depressed. He wants you experiencing His joy no matter the circumstances of your life.

Do this Exercise:

On a scale from 1-10, rate your depression: 1 – no depression; and, 10 – being very depressed.

Close your eyes and, purposely, think about the negative thoughts, helplessness and hopelessness you feel. Stay in that moment. Feel the weight of the depression. It's heavy and you have been carrying it for a long time. It feels really dark. Ask yourself, why do I feel this way? Why do I think this way? It could be you have always thought, "Things never work out for me, I'll never be happy, no one pays attention to me." Or, you may have recently acquired these thoughts. As you think those thoughts, at the same time, think about how much God loves you, how He desires you and the price He paid for you. You are His prize possession! Say this, "I am fearfully and wonderfully made." Do this as often as you think about if for two weeks; and, at the end of the two weeks – repeat the rating scale above and compare the numbers. The numbers will drop; and, you will **Overcome Depression**!

Closing thoughts...

There are many paths people take towards healing their mind and body and some of these ways effectively heal the mind and body. It is possible to be so focused on healing your mind and body that you neglect the spiritual part of you. This is not complete healing. Complete healing comes from your creator. Just like no one can fix your car like the original manufacturer, no one on this earth can bring you complete healing like your maker. God provides the kind of healing that leaves you at peace with yourself, God and man. Only your manufacturer can completely restore your body, soul and spirit.

Scriptures to help you discover the true path to healing:

I Thessalonians 5:23 (MSG): **"May God Himself, the God who makes everything holy and whole, make you holy and whole, put you together-spirit, soul and body-**

and keep you fit for the coming of our Master, Jesus Christ."

3 John 2: "Beloved I wish above all things that you prosper and be in health, even as your soul prospers."

I believe my book was written from God's heart to yours, to bring you to a place of revelation for your total healing! While God has given us awesome tools through the wisdom of man, His intention is that we would not look to those human means for healing alone, but use them in conjunction with His supernatural intervention in our lives. Knowing that He is the one who we look to in order to bring us to a place of healing and restoration.

2 Pet 1:3: "As His Divine power has given to us all things that pertain to life and godliness, through the knowledge of Him who called us by glory and virtue,"

Mark 10:27: "But Jesus looked at them and said, "With men it is impossible, but not with God; for with God all things are possible."

I love you to Life!
Regina Randolph-Davis

Chapter Excerpt from the book, *How to Overcome Anything, Tools for Living a Victorious Life*, by Regina Randolph-Davis, MSW.

INSPIRED BY LOVE

Regina Randolph Davis is a wife to her husband and partner in ministry Robert and a mother of three children she adores; Samuel, Sarai and Janae Grace. She holds a Bachelor's degree in Psychology and a Master's Degree from the University of Pennsylvania. She is a practicing Psychotherapist and along with her husband pastors Abundant Life Family Church in North Wales, Pennsylvania and Bridgewater, NJ, where they teach the word of God.

Pastor Regina is the founder of Daughters of Destiny International (DDI) the women's ministry of Abundant Life Family Church. The purpose of DDI is to empower, encourage and strengthen women to live out their God-given destiny through her dynamic teaching of the word of God and spirit-led opportunities. Such as Conferences, fellowships, and missions. Many women are drawn to her as a mentor, teacher, and counselor.

She is also the author of her first of many books "How to Overcome Anything" in this book, Pastor Regina shares her personal struggles with a debilitating illness, challenges with her emotional and spiritual health as well as her professional experiences to show you how to be set free from any mental, physical and spiritual strongholds. Through careful study of the scriptures and Pastor Regina's background in psychology, she shows the reader how to be free from and avoid the destructive patterns that keep you from enjoying and succeeding in life. She unlocks keys to defeat problems that hold you back from experiencing more in life such as anxiety, depression, fear, anger, and addictions. She is also the author of "Breaking Free" Overcoming Ungodly Soul-ties soon to be released.

By the power of the Life-Changing Gospel of Jesus Christ!

THE FIGHT

Victoria Sowell

INSPIRED BY LOVE

Ephesians 6:13-18 (MSG):

Be prepared. You're up against far more than you can handle on your own. Take all the help you can get, every weapon God has issued, so that when it's all over but the shouting; you'll still be on your feet. Truth, righteousness, peace, faith, and salvation are more than words. Learn how to apply them. You'll need them throughout your life. God's Word is an indispensable weapon. In the same way, prayer is essential in this ongoing warfare. Pray hard and long. Pray for your brothers and sisters. Keep your eyes open. Keep each other's spirits up so that no one falls behind or drops out."

You may have read, or heard of, the phrase "Your fight is not with flesh and blood," but it can be a little frustrating understanding that – especially when you are dealing with "flesh and blood" right in front of you. How can you apply this scripture to your life without someone teaching you what that means and what it, actually, looks like? Throughout my years of ministry, I've come to find that there are many crafty individuals who memorize scripture, pretending, in order to make others believe that they have both *information* and *revelation*. Truth be told, they are some of the most inconsistent and unstable when it comes to the application of scripture in their own lives.

It is imperative that you recognize that the opposition you face, as a result of the things that God has given and will give to you, is ***not*** with a physical enemy that you can see. God wants us to be prepared daily for spiritual acts of war that may try to oppose us by totally depending on Him to aid us in living a victorious life. We are no match for the enemy on our own, but with God, we are indomitable. We must remain prayerful in the midst of every situation, keep our eyes open, and become vigilant in our intercession for others. That is our mandate for preparation.

Along the journey towards destiny, you will encounter sundry obstacles that may catch you off guard. You may even wonder if you are in the twilight zone. Life happens to us all, but for some, it seems that life happens to them a bit more than it does the rest of the world. What are you going to do when it is your time of being tested, tried, and absolutely disappointed?

Don't be mistaken. There is a *Fight* over your destiny. The enemy is petrified of who you are becoming, so he wages an illegal attack against your life and expects you to just lie down and take it! Well, you are not going to do that! You are going to fight back with the good fight-of-faith! We are not fighting physical enemies; therefore, our warfare cannot be carnal or battled in the flesh.

2 Corinthians 10:4 (KJV): **⁴"For the weapons of our warfare are not carnal, but mighty through God to the pulling down of strong holds."**

It is my desire to teach you how to apply the art of loving in the midst of hatred, resistance and persecution. This chapter is designed to teach you how to fight the good fight-of-faith and enable you to effectively apply the principles necessary for you to win. You will learn how to practically apply the whole armor of God, so that when all the chaos is complete, you will be standing in poise, power, position, influence and great favor.

I, often, think back over the life-changing encounter I had with God over this past year, which seems as if it just happened on yesterday. Although it is difficult to convey the depth of the pain, heartache, disappointment and frustration I've experienced. I'd like to share some of those moments with you, along with the precious life-changing truths that The Spirit of God taught me during that time.

I was at a very low point in my life. Everything I had poured my all into seemed to be over. These were dark times for me, as, in addition to my disappointment, I experienced humiliation and shame. The agonizing stress I felt seemed to elude words. All that I had worked so hard for seemed to have vanished in one moment. My marriage, my ministry of 18 years, my position and my reputation within the community in which I served and fellowshipped were all gone. My life had taken a tailspin and began spiraling out of control. My mental state was poor, but I was somehow able to keep myself together enough to make public appearances and even minister.

Looking back even further, it seems my life has always been difficult. I was born into a family where addiction, adverse poverty, and physical abuse were commonplace. Growing up in such a situation breeds low self-esteem and makes it extremely hard for a person whose life is destined to make a positive impact in this world to fulfill their purpose. The scripture verse in *Jeremiah 29:11* became a lifeline for me as I began my walk with Christ; however, I kept running into circumstances that would cause emotions and re-occurring failures to arise. I didn't understand that what I had experienced all those years had placed indelible marks on my soul, which caused me to remember the dysfunction and attract those same things into my life.

Ephesians 6:17-18 in *The Message Bible* states that: **"God's Word is an indispensable weapon. In the same way, prayer is essential in this ongoing warfare. Pray hard and long. Pray for your brothers and sisters. Keep your eyes open. Keep each other's spirits up so that no one falls behind or drops out."**

God's Word is paramount in obtaining and maintaining your victory. There's no way around it, so you must be ready to become a student. You must STUDY to show yourself approved unto God, so that in the end you will not be made ashamed.

You will learn to enjoy a life of prayer and fellowship with God, even as you begin to realize how your prayer life, coupled with the Word and practical application, has placed you on a new playing field. You cannot do this alone, however. You will need others to come alongside you. I cannot stress that enough. You will need a team of encouragers and a very good support system. No man is an island unto himself. Even though we desire independence, God knows what is best. He wants us interdependent on each other. They will need you, but you will also need them. There are times we may choose the wrong people to be a part of our team, but with discernment, we will know – what is a Godly connection and what's not – so that we can continue to win.

Let's now focus on your mind, worth and destiny. The enemy does not want you to complete the very thing you were put into the earth to do, but he is a defeated foe and we are the victorious ones through Christ Jesus.

The two following passages from the *Bible* clearly establish the fact that man is a triune being composed of a spirit, a soul, and a body: **"I pray God your whole spirit and soul and body be preserved blameless unto the coming of our Lord Jesus Christ."** *1 Thessalonians 5:23*

"For the word of God is quick, and powerful, and sharper than any two-edged sword, piercing even to the dividing asunder of soul and spirit, and of the joints and marrow (body), and is a discerner of the thoughts and intents of the heart." *Hebrews 4:12*

I had to make the decision to apply the Word of God into my everyday life. What also helped me through the years were workbooks and devotionals that I used to supplement and enhance my understanding of the Bible. It was The Word of God that kept me alive and served as a weapon to war against the enemy – Satan. I believe it made me more dependent on God and His word, as my life was seemingly being reconstructed. I began to develop more in my gifts, talents, and abilities, but there were some things I had to learn through different stages of growth and development in life. There seemed to be times when it felt like I was on the upswing and then a new season of pain would emerge.

I moved to Orlando, Florida, in 1995. As a young Christian, there had been a myriad of issues I'd overcome in my hometown. This new transition represented a life full of new experiences and opportunities. After settling down in the area, I met a lot of good people and my pastor became like a father to me. I had always longed for a father. Even though I had a biological father, I yearned for a spiritual father that would teach me the ways of God and affirm me as a woman.

I served, faithfully, under my pastor as his personal secretary, gaining beneficial knowledge and experience that prepared me for the next steps of my life's journey. Soon, I married a man that was called by God to pastor. Not too long after we got married, my husband began pastoring a church. It was, definitely, a walk of faith, because we didn't have a congregation. We'd soon learn that our assignment to pastor would be most complex until we learned the art of praying and calling in the souls attached to our ministry assignment.

We worked, diligently, in the kingdom to build a very successful and thriving ministry. God had given us a special anointing in the areas of teaching, preaching, worship, and deliverance. Eventually, we understood that the call to apostolic and prophetic leadership rested upon our lives. Then, seemingly out of nowhere, things began to transpire; and, I found myself in a situation where I was facing divorce, all while still being called to ministry. Questions of "how could this be? What happened?" began rising within me. I loved my husband. I loved our ministry. In the end, I discovered that there was a sexual assault that had occurred, and it was the root of our marital demise. I even had to face social media warfare and rejection from many people that believed the lies that were surfacing regarding the situation. My life seemed shattered.

After my former husband left the church, I assumed the role as senior pastor. Many unresolved issues began to surface; and, it became virtually impossible for me to continue pastoring. Subsequently, the many attempts to keep the ministry functioning as normal did not work. In a state of unrest and exhaustion, I felt led to turn the ministry over to a man and woman of God, who I knew were very capable of caring for the ministry and the congregation. In order to fully heal and mend my broken spirit, I moved out of the state to get away from things that were trying to distract and discourage me. It was at that point that I started to come face-to-face with the issues involving divorce and transition. I truly understand why God hates divorce!

Man is a tripartite being. Man is a spirit because God is a spirit; and, we are made in his image *Genesis 1:26:* **"Then God said, "Let us make mankind in our image, in our likeness, so that they may rule over the fish in the sea and the birds in the sky, over the livestock and all the wild animals, and over all the creatures that move along the ground."**

He lives in a body, even as Jesus needed a body to operate legally in the earth. *Hebrews 10:5* **"Wherefore when he cometh into the world, he saith, Sacrifice and offering thou wouldest not, but a body hast thou prepared me;"** and, he possesses a soul. *Genesis 2:7:* **"And the LORD God formed man of the dust of the ground, and breathed into his nostrils the breath of life; and man became a living soul."** Man's spirit is saved and his soul must be renewed.

My soul had become fragmented, but I did not realize how badly. In understanding that my soul is comprised of my mind, will, intellect, imagination and emotions; all of those components were now off balance.

INSPIRED BY LOVE

My mind, which handles my thoughts, would overthink everything. I would second guess myself and every decision I pretended I could not believe being married to a preacher was the will of God for my life. I had fallen apart and my thoughts about God had to be governed and checked. I had to make sure not to "lose my mind," so I forced myself to go back and use the tools I learned in counseling, coupled with the Word of God.

My will was the component where I decided what I would or would not do. Once I heard from God, I had to choose to say YES. Trust me; there were so many times I did not want to say YES because it cost me so much. There were times when asked to do certain things; I'd say YES, and then go home to cry. The Word, definitely, served as a buffer for my mind and will. I learned the art of surrender.

My intellect was also challenged because I would go over into the area of reasoning. I would funnel every decision through the filter of human reasoning. In order to remain healthy in my thinking, I had to begin funneling things through the Word of God. The Word of God was my litmus test to help me determine what I needed to meditate on or take at face value.

My emotions were damaged the most. I would cry at any given time, for no reason at all. Watching a story on television or even seeing the people who were in my previous ministry would trigger negative emotions. I realized I needed to take a timeout and walk out my healing.

Of course, Jesus had already healed me, but I'm sharing my process in walking it through.

Romans 12:2: ***"Be not conformed to this world but be transformed by the renewing of your mind that you may prove what is that good and acceptable and perfect will of God."***

In order for me to walk into my total healing, I had to really meditate on the above scripture and understand that real change happens in the soul of a man. In order for anyone to experience transformation, they must master the art of mind renewal or changing how they process information, pain, trials, etc. We must meditate on the Word according to *Joshua 1:8:* ***"This book of the law shall not depart out of thy mouth; but thou shalt meditate therein day and night, that thou mayest observe to do according to all that is written therein: for them thou shalt make thy way prosperous and then thou shalt have good success."***

To meditate, means to think deeply or focus one's mind for a period of time, in silence or with the aid of chanting or to mutter. When a thought comes that is contrary to the

Word of God, we must cast it down, according to *2 Corinthians 10:5-6:* **"⁵Casting down imaginations, and every high thing that exalts itself against the knowledge of God, and bringing into captivity every thought to the obedience of Christ; ⁶And having in a readiness to revenge all disobedience when your obedience is fulfilled."**

The journey to healing requires you to submit to the transformation process by challenging the thoughts that are contrary to the Word of God. Meditating requires you to say something, and that something should be the Word of God. You must cast down every imagination, making it obey the Word of God and punish every thought that rebels, by applying what you know the Word says.

For example, let's take an evil thought or lie of the devil – "No one will ever truly love me" – and cast it down by replacing it with this declaration: "I cast down that evil thought and bring it captive to the Word of God, according to *John 3:16*: **"that God loved me so much he gave his only begotten son for me that I might have everlasting life."**

By making that declaration, you have resisted the opportunity to be conformed to this world's system, and you have now begun a transformation process in your mind. Through meditation, you are making your way prosperous, and good success is headed in your direction.

So, when you begin to think: "I AM LOVED," everything in your life will start to conform to your most dominant thought. Healing and transformation require that you do your part.

Mindset Following Divorce

I finally saw what the *Bible* meant about having our minds renewed truly looked like. Overcoming the thoughts of unworthiness and rejection that normally accompany divorce required some serious fighting. The enemy would love to use the failure of a marriage to destroy anyone he can. My thinking about the situation had to change. I had to remember the numerous amounts of hours spent in counseling trying to save my marriage and the tools presented to help me with my raging soul.

I was reminded that if my soul didn't prosper, I wouldn't prosper.

2 John 3 (KJV): **"Beloved, I wish above all things that thou mayest prosper and be in health even as your soul prosper."**

I had to guard my thoughts. I had to become proficient at the art of casting down imaginations and exchange those negative thoughts for the Word of God. My thinking had to change about myself. I had to remind myself daily that "I am loved." The enemy was using the situation to tear me apart. I needed people to love me unconditionally. It was then that I, finally, realized how badly I needed people in my life. At times in my life I thought I was independent and, really, didn't need anyone but Jesus. Well, the song that says *"As long as I've got King Jesus, I don't need nobody else"* is FALSE! You WILL need someone, as you will quickly discover – in the midst of real trial and testing. I, quickly, let go of that independent spirit and started embracing those God brought into my life.

In this process, I discovered that the love I was receiving was literally God loving me through these people. Every act of kindness and love I received I attributed to God in his mercy and grace for me. I knew that if I was ever granted another chance to love or receive love, that it would be a gift from God himself. He loves me through people, and He will love you through people too!

The Holy Spirit is the comforter according to *John 14:16:* **"And I will pray the Father, and he shall give you another Comforter, that he may abide with you forever."** God did not leave me alone in the earth to fight. He made sure that Jesus left me a "Helper" – one that is called alongside me. He is the third person of the Trinity; and, his assignment is to make sure that I get through this life victoriously. He leads and guides us by speaking to our hearts when we acknowledge and ask for his help. I also want you to learn as I have that his ministry is valid and needed to overcome the wiles of the devil.

INSPIRED BY LOVE

God gives us both the Holy Spirit and other people to aid us in our healing process. We are not alone! We have everything we need to survive the seasons we face in our lives. My mindset following divorce is that God loves me unconditionally. He gives me the grace to overcome my issues and whatever happens to me! This too shall pass!

When Things Are Out of Your Control

You are in a good place when things are out of your control. Life is not meant to be controlled. I spent most of my life trying to control what happened to me. I tried to control everybody else's life around me, too and found out that neither life nor people and their situations can be controlled. It is offensive when you are a person that likes to be in control and then God takes away what you thought you had control over. He will close every avenue that you are accustomed to following, in order to get your attention. He does not want you in charge; He wants you to relinquish your hold on your life and trust HIM. To trust God means to place confidence in, to be assured by, certain of, and reliant on Him. In essence, it is the reliability, truth, ability or strength of God.

When my life began to spiral out of control, despite my trying to figure out how to make things better, everything only got worse. I became an emotional wreck. I preached about trust but realized that my foundation was not properly founded on really trusting in the true and living God. An example of trust is found in *Matthew 14:22-33*. Jesus has his disciples to get on a boat headed to the other side. Later, in that same scripture, Jesus appears to his disciples and is walking on the water. When the disciples see him, they are terrified. Jesus tells them not to be afraid. All were silent; but Peter intriguingly asks Jesus if he could come join him in the phenomenon, and he, too, begins walking on the water. It took an amazing level of trust to defy the laws of nature and walk on water. Peter walked on water based on the word of Jesus when he said, "Come." Even while experiencing a walk-on-water miracle, Peter takes his focus off of Jesus and looks at the wind and water, becomes afraid, and immediately begins to sink.

Similarly, when my life was out of control, I took my focus off of God and looked instead at my situation, which looked hopeless. All the years of working and laboring in the gospel began blowing fiercely, like the wind, when things began falling apart in my marriage and ministry. It felt as though the winds were forcing me to leave my city and so many of the people I loved dearly like I had no other choice. The situation was out of my control. I was unable to handle the adversity I was facing alone. I needed time to heal, and now it was my time to receive ministry, so I had to make the decision to seek help for myself. Now that it was all out of my control I knew I had let it all die. I was afraid. Fear gripped my life and produced hopelessness. Depression and heaviness surrounded me. I'd like to pretend that I handled it like a champ, but I didn't.

God then gave me this scripture: *John 12:24:* ***"Verily, verily I say unto you, Except a corn of wheat fall into the ground and die, it abideth alone: and if it die, it remains by itself. But if it die, it bringeth forth much fruit."*** God said to me, "Let it all die" and my heart broke. Then he told me, "I'll give it back to you better. You'll be better in ministry because of this – because the fruit that has been cultivated and developed places you in a new place. You will produce much fruit."

It did not look like fruit was being produced. I would cry aloud to the Lord: "I am over 50 years old; how can I start over again?" He repeated, "Let it die." I did not see God as a good, good father. I felt He was being unfair to me; but, fortunately, the Holy Spirit and his ministry began to speak louder than my soul. It goes back to the transformation process and how I had to live it day in and day out until this thing broke off of my life. Just as Jesus rebuked Peter for his lack of faith, he also rebuked me. I had to check my foundation of faith and begin to fight using the Word, with tears streaming down my face. Sometimes it took hours; sometimes it took days, and some situations took months. Honestly, even now, layers are daily being revealed, and the healing is a process for me.

Isolation for Healing

By definition, "quarantine" is a strict isolation imposed to prevent the spread of disease or infection. For some people, this extreme measure of healing isn't necessary, but for me, isolation was necessary. In the medical world, a decision on where to put you regarding recovery is based on the intensity of the wounds (Intensive Care Unit, Critical Care Unit, and in extreme cases Isolation Units). Isolation from human interaction is, definitely, not healthy for long periods of time; but, in rare cases, isolation has been deemed both necessary and beneficial. Isolation becomes necessary in situations where your wounds are highly contagious and when the sensitivity of your wound can be adversely affected by human interactions, or in cases when people or situations can cause an upset in one's mental state.

There are times that God will quarantine you or isolate you for short periods of time while He digs out the infection and pours in the revelation of His love. He does not want anything or anyone to be able to spread the infectious pain going on in your soul to the other parts of the body. He especially needed my heart to be protected while the cutting, digging, and pressing was taking place at heaven's command. It would not look like the work of a loving father if the wrong voices spoke into the situation, causing their issue to spread and releasing the venom of issues that remain unresolved in them."

The only voices that were able to speak to me for several months were the Word of God and the Precious Holy Spirit. I had to pray, worship, read the Word and work through my process. I, now realize, that God isolated me so he could have those months alone with me. You may ask, "Where were you?" I was on 100 acres of beautiful real estate that my leaders allowed me to go away to heal. The horses and deer became my friends. The Word was my medication and meditation. The Holy Spirit would help me to understand the time and season I was in.

Now, the isolation is over and the imminent danger is no more. I say as the psalmist David, "It was good for me that I was afflicted." Trust me; I have learned much through this ordeal. I have a greater love and compassion for people. Specifically, women in ministry – who are a great concern – because this level of pain affects so many areas of your life.

Women, you must acknowledge when you need help so that you can be healed. We need to hear your story. You survived what others may have killed themselves over. That in and of itself is a gift to you. Thank God you have your health, strength, and mind. Many people break at this place. You did not. You survived, and there is much work for you to do!

Willing to Walk Away From It All to Pursue God

I've seen almost everything imaginable happen in church, after spending several years in ministry and pastoring for 18 years. I have survived much of it in order to share with you the valuable principles in "The Fight." My decision to walk away was based on several factors; one being – the level of adversity and fight I was facing; and, the obvious other, being – the pain of divorce; and, most importantly, the leading of the Holy Spirit. I asked the question so many times before: "What do you do when the trial you are facing isn't coming from the devil?" Walking away from people whom I loved was the single most difficult decision of my life. Letting something go after sowing so many years and waiting for the harvest to manifest is more difficult than you can imagine. I knew it was best for me and I knew it was best for the people, but my emotional tie to them was the trial I faced.

I realized that pursuing God in this new place required my total obedience. Even if I did not understand why or what He was doing in my life, I had to trust Him beyond anything I have had to rely on in times past. It was the ultimate sacrifice.

Hebrews 13:15 (KJV): **"By him therefore let us offer the sacrifice of praise to God continually, that is, the fruit of our lips giving thanks to his name."**

The situation pushed me into understanding what a real offering looked like. Sacrifice is the act of giving up something that you want to keep – especially, in order to get or do something else or to please God. That became my motivation for pushing and pressing. I wanted to please God and make him happy, so I would offer the sacrifice of praise and thanksgiving even when I wanted to be sad, ungrateful, and depressed. I must say, there were many days when sadness, disappointment, and depression had its hold on me; but, thank God for His amazing grace! He would strengthen me to get through each obstacle and allow me to start over the next day with new mercies. It seemed as if the season would last forever; but, I held on to the promise that God would give me the desires of my heart and he wouldn't withhold anything good from me as indicated in *Psalm 37:4:* **"Delight thyself also in the Lord; and he shall give thee the desires of thine heart"** and *Psalm 84:11:* **"For the Lord God is a sun and shield: the Lord will give grace and glory: no good thing will he withhold from them that walk uprightly."**

These scriptures became an anchor for me. I began to meditate on them, mutter them, add them to my prayers and use them to put faith pressure in the atmosphere and that's when things started to break. The Word became my confession, thanksgiving and meditation added to my prayers. The Word became a part of the promise declared, and it cemented me into a place of trust. Even on days when the same doubt, fear, rejection and other negative emotions would arise because of delay, I would remember the anchor that was holding me in place to receive all that God has for me.

My process continues, but I would not trade anything or ask God to omit that part of my story. I embrace it and choose to believe that my latter days will be better than my former; that God is rebuilding my life, and that my future is bright. I can, wholeheartedly, say that I have true joy, unspeakable and full of glory! I now know the peace that comes as a result of a promise made and all I had to do was relax and receive it! I look forward to the opportunity to share my story around the globe and help be a part of the healing many people need. Most of all, I would like to be what I needed in my situation – a helper to others in their situation – by really coaching them and laying these powerful truths in front of them as they evolve and begin to live again.

INSPIRED BY LOVE

1 Peter 4:12-13: *[12]"**Beloved think it not strange concerning the fiery trial which is to try you as though some strange thing happened unto you: [13]But rejoice, inasmuch as ye are partakers of Christ's sufferings; that, when his glory shall be revealed ye may be glad also with exceeding joy."*

Lastly, things are going to happen to you. Life happens to us all. It is, really, how we process those things that happen to us that determines our outcome. There are trials, and there are fiery trials. At any rate, we must rest assured that we will all have our turn to deal with them. It is comforting to know that we are partaking of Christ's sufferings and His glory shall be revealed as we rejoice. We are counted worthy to suffer so that His glory can be revealed in the situations we face. He believes that we will accept the challenge and trust the process.

Whatever you are facing today, rejoice and know that God is a good father and He has all things under control. He will NEVER leave you alone. He is ALWAYS there, regardless of where your "there" may be. I like to say it like many songwriters have before me: "There shall be glory after this!" It sounds like just a good catch-phrase or nice song lyric – until the fiery trials of your life try to consume you. Then, those words become a revelatory point of reference reminding you that it is not over yet. There will be times of temptation, but don't give in. There is no temptation worth forfeiting all that God has for you. There will be others who will come along and tell you to give up or do it another way but don't do it. God has a plan. His plan is good; and, if you continue to trust, you will know His goodness and see His faithfulness. God loves you with an everlasting love and His intentions toward you are always good.

Go ahead and brag about His goodness before you see the results manifested. A real sacrifice of praise causes you to praise God, unreservedly, without seeing any outcome; but, with the assurance that the very nature of God will manifest. He is good all the time. He is faithful all the time. He cannot lie, and He will not fail. That is what makes Him so mighty – He is not like man! Take time over this day to really offer him the best offering you have – the sacrifice of praise! You know why? Because you WIN. You win the fight!

2 Corinthians 2:14 (KJV): **"Now thanks be unto God who always causes us to triumph in Christ, and maketh manifest the savior of his knowledge by us in every place."**

2 Corinthians 2:14 (ERV): **"But thanks be to God, who always leads us into victory through Christ. God uses us to spread his knowledge everywhere like a sweet-smelling perfume."**

INSPIRED BY LOVE

2 Corinthians 2:14 (AMP): **"But thanks be to God, Who in Christ always leads us in triumph [as trophies of Christ's victory] and through us spreads and makes evident the fragrance of knowledge of God everywhere."**

2 Corinthians 2:14 (MSG): **"And I got it, thank God! in the Messiah, in Christ, God leads us from place to place in one perpetual victory parade. Through us, he brings knowledge of Christ. Everywhere we go people breath in the exquisite fragrance."**

2 Corinthians 2:14 (VOICE): **"Yet I am thankful to God, who always marches us to victory under the banner of the Anointed One; and through us He spreads the beautiful fragrance of His knowledge to every corner of the earth."**

So, regardless of which translation you read, it clearly indicates your status – you are victorious, and you win! Not only that, you leave a sweet fragrance or aroma in the atmosphere!

INSPIRED BY LOVE

Dr. Sowell has been placed in the marketplace and is being used to share the gospel in various financial arenas. This profound entrepreneur has several initiatives already in place such as CEO of several nonprofit organizations. With these organizations, she has begun and continue to oversee a private school for over 13 years, a hair salon, & a family preservation center.

Graduates of Victory Prep Christian Academy are giving an opportunity to jump-start their careers by becoming staff for the private school or starting their hair business in her salon and many other opportunities to gain valuable on the job training.

The Love Outreach Center is also a part of one of her nonprofits that reaches women that have been caught up in sexual trafficking it is a year-long residential program. Also, provide housing for women in transition.

In addition, Dr. Victoria takes time to mentor numerous young ladies on business ethics, inner healing, and spiritual growth. Her heart and love for to see women set free and healed is a heartfelt passion.

Dr. Victoria Sowell is a Virtuous Woman, an author, songwriter and singer that you usher you into the presence of God and your life will change.

PRAYING FOR YOUR SPOUSE

Angela Thornton

First of all, then, I urge that entreaties and prayers, petitions and thanksgivings, be made on behalf of all men. ~1 Timothy 2:1 (NASB)

[14] This is the confidence which we have before Him, that, if we ask anything according to His will, He hears us. [15] And if we know that He hears us in whatever we ask, we know that we have the requests which we have asked from Him. ~1 John 5:14-15 (NASB)

Marriage is beautiful. In fact, it is one of the most dynamic things God ever created. Its purpose is to unite two individuals, binding them together, through their love and commitment, making them one. God, in His infinite wisdom, decided there would be no other relationship on earth that can compare to the intimacy of marriage as He designed it. Nothing else can come close to the beauty of the love a husband has for his wife, and she has for him. Perhaps that is why Satan fights so hard to destroy the first institution God created. Maybe that is why he spends so much time attempting to make us believe that love is not a many splendored thing. Love is the foundation of any union. God ordains it by the power of His love. God sustains it by the power of His Word. And Prayer upholds it.

INSPIRED BY LOVE

Love is beautiful. Love is kind. It does not get jealous, neither is it proud. Love never gives up or loses faith. Love is always hopeful. Love will endure through every circumstance. Love will last forever. It is why everyone wants to be loved. We were not made to be alone. We were not made to be an island. We were created to be in loving relationships with one another. The *Bible* shows us in *Genesis* that everything God created, he made two of after their own kind. Even God, Himself, was not alone; for He said, **"let us make man in OUR image and according to OUR likeness."**

Most of us want to be married. Rare is the person who wants to be alone. It is, seemingly, not natural to be alone. How do we know? *Genesis 2:18* tells us the Lord said, **"It is not good for the man to be alone; I will make him a helper suitable for him."** What I love about God is that He gives what He knows we need, even when we do not necessarily see it. For instance, Adam didn't know he was alone. Adam didn't know he NEEDED a companion. Imagine that; you are the very thing he NEEDS.

When God made Eve in *Gen 2:21-22*, by the time He "took" her to Adam, she was perfect. She was EVERYTHING he needed. She was everything he wanted. She was PERFECT for him.

Verse 23 tells us that Adam was beyond excited. Here what he said in *Genesis 2:23-24,* "*²³The man said,* "This is *now bone of my bones, And flesh of my flesh; She shall be called Woman, Because she was taken out of Man." ²⁴For this reason a man shall leave his father and his mother, and be joined to his wife, and they shall become one flesh.*

To that end, if we are going to have successful relationships, they must be based in, rooted in, grounded in, and formed around the word of the Lord. Yes, I know that there are many successful relationships with people who are not believers in Christ. But, if you say that you are a Christ follower then your relationship must be according to His word and His will. The only way to make sure that is the case is to bathe that relationship in His word and prayer. I have discovered that prayer is a unique and divine gift God gave us so that we have direct access to His throne room to communicate with Him.

If we pray the word, then God is obligated to answer, because it is His word that forever is settled in heaven. When our focus is on the Lord, so too will the desire of our heart. We won't ask anything that is outside of His will. And so, when we desire what God wants for us, it is the absolute best for us. For instance, we may want a mate to have specific physical characteristics, to have accomplished certain material things; to live in a particular way and drive a particular type of car. [*Side note: I speak from experience.*] I wanted a man who was tall, slim, well-dressed, well-educated, well-traveled and blessed with a milk chocolate complexion just like my daddy.

The man God chose for me is short, not at all slim, drove a burnt orange Chevy *Chevette*, and was not well-dressed and worked at *Pizza Hut* when we met. But here's what he did have, he met every criteria for how I wanted to be treated; even though he did not meet my external requirements. God spoke and said all those things I wanted are superficial and they are temporal. Please know I'm not saying to you that you must go out and find "Omar, The Ogre." I'm not saying that you need to find the most unattractive person on this side of glory to have a fruitful and loving relationship.

What I am saying is the foundation of your relationship cannot be based on what the person looks like, possesses or has the potential to become. That requires prayer and asking the Lord, "God, who do you have for me? Make me and shape me into the person, the woman or the man that you would have me to be, so that I may attract the person that you have created just for me." You may ask, "How can I do that?" It will happen through prayer and Bible Study. It will happen because of your obedience to God.

Once you have met that person, you must pray for them. In fact, you must pray for them before you ever know them. Because when you meet them, your spirit will bear witness to what you have been praying because it would have been according to God's word. Yes, like spirits indeed attract, and water seeks its own level.

Let's be very – clear you cannot pray for someone else's husband, or wife, and believe that God is going to bless that. I can assure you He is not. Likewise, you cannot pray that someone else's relationship will end because you think that's the person you want. It's not going to happen. But how then do I pray for my mate? What do I pray?

First, search the Scriptures to find out what God says a good husband or a good wife is. What does that person look like? How does he feel to me? What does that person enjoy? Who am I to be – to them? Who were they to be – to me? What are we to do – together? How do we fit into each other's life? What is it that we are supposed to do? What impact are we supposed to make? Once we know that and have it all laid out, then we can craft our prayers according to God's word and his will.

Here's what I know, you attract what you are. You draw who you are. God didn't present Eve to Adam until he was fully prepared to receive her, and she was whole and ready to be received. Too often, we get caught up in someone's potential and fail to see who they are right now.

If a good man is what you want, be sure you are a good woman. Pray that the Lord would prepare you to be what your future or current husband needs. Pray that God has taught him how to treat you, how to love you, how to cover you. Pray that the Lord has prepared him to be the priest, provider, and protector of your home. Pray that he is not the walking wounded, still bleeding from hurts of past relationships. Can he cook, clean and keep a healthy, happy, peaceful home? Is he committed to pray with and for you and your family? Will he lead you in Bible study or must we depend on the Church alone? In essence, is he the thermostat or the thermometer of your home?

Ask yourself some questions, and ask God to give you insight and discernment for the answers. Is he whole or is he still walking around with unhealed and unresolved issues? Is he looking for a "better half?" I would hope not because if he is, might I ask, where the other "half" is coming from? Because the *Bible* says "and the TWO become one" (not the two halves became one). Does he want a wife or is he looking for another mother or a maid? Do you want another father or someone to rescue you? Is he as committed to loving you as Christ loved the Church?

To get the answers you need, will require much prayer. Interceding for your husband, or husband to be, is essential to having a thriving marriage and to seeing Gods power in your union. Praying for your husband is both a privilege and necessity. God longs to show us compassion. He wants us to pour out our heart and bring our concerns for those we love. Praying Scripture over your husband is one of the best ways to bless him, because it is both practical and prophetic. Our desire for them should be like what God spoke to the children of Israel in *Ezekiel 34:26:* ***"I will bless them and the places surrounding my hill. I will send down showers in season; there will be showers of blessing."***

If you want to protect and cover your marriage, engage in consistent prayer. There is, almost, no better way to show your love and care for your husband. Regular and sustained prayer has the power to transform your marriage. What's crooked can be made straight. What's broken can be fixed. What's lacking can be fulfilled. When you pray for your spouse, you are, in essence, saying, when the going gets tough, I will pray more and talk less.

If you wonder why you should pray without ceasing for your spouse, here are a few reasons:

(1) **Praying for him will unite you spiritually**. Praying for him will bring you into an agreement and lessen the times you major in the minor. It will help you not get bogged down in the minutiae and see the big picture for your marriage and family. Praying for and with him will knit your hearts such that you become as one heart and one soul with the two genuinely becoming one.

(2) **Praying for him will encourage humility and honesty in both of you**. Trust me, becoming a unified team is not a given after you say I do. You are melding two personalities, backgrounds, life experiences and set of expectations. When you pray with, and for your husband, it enables both of you to trust each other enough, to be honest about your weaknesses and shortcomings and to show your vulnerabilities. Because guess what as in love as you might be, the shine eventually wears off and you need to have laid a foundation to deal with the less than pretty parts of marriage.

(3) **Praying for and with him helps you to develop and deepen your ability to communicate**. Open and honest communication is a fundamental key to genuine companionship and prayer is the key that opens the door. Praying for your husband helps you gain a deeper understanding of who he is and what he needs. You will learn what is on your husband's heart through prayer and he will learn what's in yours as well. If there is a hiccup in your marriage, you may not be able to say everything you feel to your husband, but with God, you can bare your soul. Your intercession with God will give you strategies on how to communicate with your husband.

(1) **Prayer will establish deeper intimacy and companionship**. Ponder for a minute. What are the primary issues that hinder real companionship and intimacy with your spouse? Mainly, it is a lack of communication and often pride. As you humbly go to God praying for your marriage, you will be changed. You will automatically grow spiritually and become more unified. Lest we forget, companionship is an important reason we marry. I daresay, the closer you get to God, the closer you will be with your dearly beloved.

(2) **Praying for your husband will build both of you up**. Petitioning God on your husband's behalf with prayer and supplication is never a losing situation. In fact, you can't lose. Jude 1:20 says we are to build ourselves up on our most holy faith praying in the Holy Spirit. As you spend time talking with God about your marriage, He will build you up. He is, after all, your heavenly Father who says if you seek first His kingdom and righteousness, He will add all other things to you.

We are admonished to pray for our spouses. It is, equally, wise that during our season of singleness that we pray for our future spouse. If we are praying for a FUTURE spouse, perhaps we can focus our prayers on these topics:

- Pray for their health and well-being.
- Pray that they become all that God has created them to be and that they will love you as Christ has ordained.
- Pray for their mind, their physical stamina.
- You must pray for them BEFORE you ever meet them because when he finds you, he finds a wife, even though you are not yet married.
- Once you're married, you can still pray for those same things, but you must add to the list.

During my years of singleness, after my divorce, I wasn't sure I wanted to be married again. In prayer one day, as I was deciding if I wanted to marry again; or, if I wanted just to stay single; the Lord reminded me that I was doing a whole lot of contemplating on what I wanted, and very little on what He had planned for me. I never asked God if it was His will for me to remain single. I had not asked Him if it was His will that I marry my husband, Daniel. And, I certainly didn't ask if I should have married my first husband. Here's what happens when we move in our own will and don't ask the creator. We end up with mess, heartache and often disappointment and divorce. Yep, I stopped and listened to the voice of Holy Spirit; and, here's what He said,

"Pray for the one I have given you to love. Not the one you like or lust after. Not the one that suits your list, but the one that fits My purpose and plan for you."

I remembered something I once said during a single's conference – if what I had always had in the way of boyfriends and significant others had been what I had always wanted, I would not have had to have more than one of them.''

Not only should you pray FOR your spouse, but you should also pray WITH your spouse. We must pray beyond the obvious (health, strength, finances, etc.). We must pray that for the person they are right now, right in front of you AND for the potential they can become. Pray that their love of Christ saturates not just their heart, but the core of their being.

Effectively praying for your spouse means you see them as God sees them, not as you wish them to be. I had to learn; my husband is God's son. He's God's creation, not mine. So, no matter how much I wanted him to act; or, what I wanted him to become – ultimately, it was NOT my decision, it was – and is – ALL in God's hand.

Daily, I say, "Thank You, Lord, for this man you caused to find me." Thank God for the person He created just for you! I once heard a wife say, "I was created to be

His helpmate; and, he was created to be my husband, lover, and friend."

Praying for your spouse, allows you see them beyond the natural; and, instead, see who they were created to be in the spirit. Your prayers can elevate him to unimaginable heights or bring him to desperate lows. Your prayers can build him up or tear him down. Your prayers can sustain him or drain him. Your prayers can speak death over him or bring forth life in him.

Because, seriously, Sis, you can't pray for him with a sincere heart and still be mad at him. I have discovered that as I pray for my husband, God opens my eyes to see the husband He created, not the one that may be looking back at me. The Lord allows me to feel unconditional love and understand his infinite potential for good. Knowing this, brings a more profound revelation to the purpose of our union and it gives me a deeper insight into our relationship. Trust me, frustration with him and disappointment with him can't last long if you are earnestly praying for him. The Lord will often use your time of intercession on your husband's behalf to remind you just how special he is.

Now that we know we MUST pray, WHY we should pray, now what exactly SHOULD we pray? As you pray for your spouse, here are a few things to consider:

INSPIRED BY LOVE

Thank God for your husband (James 1:17)

- It is important to express gratitude to God for your spouse. Thanking God for your spouse and the unique characteristics he has that bless your life or small gestures he does for you causes your love for him to grow and mature.

- As you thank God for him, be sure to pray for things you know he needs. At times I pray for my husband and the blessings I think he needs or things he may struggle with, I feel closer to him. I feel God moving when I call on him to cover my husband or extend His hand of mercy or grace. Trusting God enough to petition Him on your spouse's behalf, shows you have faith in the Lord's ability to remove or ease the burden and solve the problem.

Pray to be a better spouse (Proverbs 12:4)

- Even after two decades of marriage, I am not a perfect wife. Sometimes my time and energy are drained from work and ministry, and my love tank is near empty. I have learned that depending on the Lord in all things, including being a good wife, is helpful. The more I pray for him, the more affectionate and selfless I become. Other times I seek the Lord to know how best to serve my husband. Then I look for answers to my prayers and ways to put my faith to the test by acting on inspiration I receive.

Pray for his heart (Proverbs 4:23)
- I don't mean his physical heart, but that is heart if for God and the things of God. Pray that he has a teachable spirit and that his ears are always open to discern and hear the voice of the Lord. As you pray for his heart, ask the Lord to protect it from unnecessary stress, pain, attacks and all temptations.

Pray for His Mind (Colossians 3:2)
- Pray that the mind that is in Christ Jesus be in him. Pray that he has a renewed and transformed mind. Pray that the decisions he makes are wise and that his choices are perceived through the lens of what is biblically sound. Pray that if there is any foolishness in his mind, God will remove it. Pray that any obstacles that would keep him from being humble and compassionate will be removed. Pray that he neither depression or oppression will come upon him.

Pray for His health and safety (1 Corinthians 3:16)
- Pray that he has a long life and good health and that he develops habits to ensure both his mind and body are fit. Ask God to show you how you can help him become and remain healthy in every area of his life. Pray for his safety and productiveness at work. Cover him as he travels to and from work or other activities. Pray that the abundant peace of God

would surpass his understanding and that the eternal favor of God would surround him as a shield.

Pray for His Purpose (Ephesians 1:11)

- Ask the Lord to reveal to your husband or husband to be what his purpose is and why he was created. Pray that daily he is encouraged and that the Lord will bring into divine alignment everything he will need to fulfill his Kingdom assignment and to walk in destiny. Pray against any feelings of insecurity, inadequacy, and unworthiness. Pray against anything that would come to derail his destiny. Ask the Lord to intercept anything meant to distract him from his purpose and disrupt the path He has set before him.

Pray that He is a Good Steward (1 Corinthians 4:1)

- Pray that he is a good steward not just of money, but of his time, his talent and all that God provides. Ask the Lord to send wise counselors who can teach, lead and guide your husband. Thank God that your husband will make wise decisions as it relates to your household finances and resources. Pray that his conviction is for your family to live debt free and leave a legacy and inheritance for your children or those connected to you.

Pray for His future (Psalm 105:42-45)

- Pray that the Lord will enlarge his territory. Ask God to reveal every dream hidden in his heart. Pray that his highest hopes and aspirations come to fruition. Pray that for every vision God gives your husband, the provision is manifested. Prat that the abundance the Lord will pour out will be shared to bless others. Yes, pray that the Lord will do exceeding, abundantly above all he could ask or imagine.

Pray for His Career and Business (Proverbs 22:29)

- Ask the Lord to bless the work of his hands. Pray that his labor will not be in vain and that it will bring forth success, prosperity, sufficient grace for the assignment and divine favor. Pray that his work will bring him great fulfillment. Ask the Lord to guide him, strengthen him and give him a vision for the future. Pray that he gives the trajectory of his career or business to the Lord. Ask God to open doors of opportunity that no man can shut and close every door that is for your spouse. Pray that he is like a tree planted by living waters that will prosper in season, always bearing good fruit and never wither.

Pray for His Walk with God (Deuteronomy 5:33)

- Pray that he thrives in ministry and intimacy with the Lord. Pray that in all things, even those concerning you, he puts God first. Ask God to teach him to spend time with him and that he continues to grow in the Word.

My final thought is this, pray without ceasing for your husband. It doesn't matter if he is a seasoned saint or a new believer, he needs your prayers. Your greatest support to him is to pray for and with him consistently. You are in covenant with him, not competition. As you pray for him, your prayers become like a force field that protects him.

Praying for your husband is honorable in the sight of the Lord. There is absolutely no one else who can intercede for him as you can. Why because you know him. You know what's in his heart. You know his fears. You know what worries him and what brings him joy. You are his best friend and his best advocate. You know him like no other person on earth. Who else can bombard the gates of heaven on his behalf better than you? No one.

When he is burdened with work or his business, you can pray for him. You may not be able to fix the problem or solve the issue, but you can pray that the peace of God will reign in his heart and mind. You can pray that the Lord will give him divine wisdom and understanding regarding what his next move should be. *Jeremiah 33:3* tells us that when we call on the Lord, He will answer and show us great and mighty things, which we do not know. Therefore, come boldly before the throne of God on behalf of your husband.

Praying for your husband changes him – and you. If during the times you have disagreements, pray that the Lord will make his heart sensitive toward you and see where he has hurt your feelings. God is faithful to answer your request. It is His good desire that you have a godly, loving and fruitful marriage. He longs for the two not just to become one, but to remain as one. Finally, if there is sin in his life, it is your responsibility to cover him in prayer asking the Lord to cleanse his heart and cause him to repent and turn back to God.

I would encourage you not to pray for your husband's heart just to get your way; no, my Sister, that is manipulation. Pray for his heart so that the two of you are drawn closer together. Remember, the effective, fervent prayer of a righteous woman (or man) will avail much. Pray that you always make him feel that he is indeed the head; just remember, you are the neck. Sis, we have never seen a head turn without the neck. The two are interwoven and dependent on each other. God has so much to give, but we must ask. As you seek the Lord according to His word, sit back and watch the fruit of your fervent and effective prayer overflow. Be encouraged. Know that your husband needs you and the power and grace of your intercession on his behalf.

INSPIRED BY LOVE

Prayer for Your Spouse

Father, make me the person I'm supposed to be as my spouse's mate. Create, in me, the heart that will attract the man you have created for me. Cause him to find me. Let the scent of me to be as pheromones in the atmosphere that only he can sense, and smell; such that our spirits will indeed knit together, and our hearts are united as one; and, that we would see each other in the spirit realm.

God, I pray now for his mind, for his heart, and his spirit. I pray for his finances and his business acumen. I pray that the work of his hands and his labor is blessed. Father, I lift before You, the desires of my husband's heart as he walks upright before You. Thank You that all that my husband needs – You will supply according to Your riches in glory. Father, I pray that the husband you've fashioned, chosen and created, just for me in heaven, will be the priest, provider, and protector of our home on earth.

I thank you that this person, this man of God, my covering, that you're sending my way – is ready – because he has been prepared for me. He knows that You have put me in the perfect place, so that he would find me. For Your Word declares that **he who finds a wife, finds a good thing and obtains favor from the Lord.** *Let me be the one who will cause your favor to fall fresh upon him. Let me be the good thing that he has found. Let me be the one with the* *remedy for whatever aches him and yes God, let me be the one who will calm his fears.*

Let being in my presence be peace to him, bring joy to his soul and happiness to the depths of his being. I thank You, Lord, that I am the one who when he sees me, his heart skips a beat just as it was for Solomon when he saw the Shulamite woman. I thank You, Father, that everything about me is attractive to him. Whatever size I am is appealing to him. I am his desire, and he is mine – in the name of Jesus. I thank you, Lord, that I am that which he both desires and needs physically. I am the one who can fill him, physically, as you fill him, spiritually, in the name of Jesus. I am the one who causes his heart to flutter, and his eyes to light up as Fourth of July *fireworks brighten up the sky. I am the one to whom you have called him to wed.*

I am the one with whom he can build a future. I am the one with whom You united to see his hopes and dreams and the fulfillment of his purpose as he walks toward his destiny. I am the one who will encourage him when life beats him down. I am the one who will tell him you can go forth – in the name of Jesus. I am the one who can inspire him, like no other, because I am his helpmeet who is bone of his bone and flesh of his flesh. I was fashioned to be just what he needs to have intimate and satisfying relations. Yes, I was made for him alone. Thank You, God, that I am the one, the bride that you have sent his way. I am that one; and, in the name of Jesus, there is no other.

I know the enemy will send an imposter, but they will all fall by the wayside, and the trick and distraction will be exposed. There will be a counterfeit. The enemy will send one who looks like me. He will send one who sounds like me. He will send one who pretends to be me, but you will show him clearly that she is not the one. You will tell him that there is another. So, Father, I give You great praise. And I give You glory, knowing that I will cover him as You cover us. I will lift him up. I will bear his burdens. I will love him. I will like him. I will protect him. I will protect his anointing. I will pray for him, and I will pray with him.
I will have his back in all that I do and in all that I say. I have his back because I know that You have mine. I am confident that what You have put together, shall never be pulled asunder, for greater is He that is in us – than he that is in the world. Thank You, Lord, that no man or woman can break this three-strand cord which You have knitted together. Finally, Father, I give You praise and glory. I praise You for the one You have created, chosen and called to find me in the name of Jesus.

INSPIRED BY LOVE

Elder Angela Thornton is a storyteller. A child of God. Wife. Mom. Mentor. Friend. I am all of these, and my desire is to live in such a way that no matter which one you meet, you will see the Word of Christ dwelling richly in me. I want my teaching to empower people to know the truth and power of God's Word that sets them free. I want my praying and interceding to be so powerful that before I call, the Lord has already sent an answer.

It is why I love the Bible. I love Jesus Christ. I love to pray. Words are my friends; hence, I write, I teach, and I speak. I love cooking and baking, which means we always have a house full of friends and family around our dinner table. My husband makes me smile and laugh until my stomach hurts. My children are living life as young adults (hallelujah). I am a southern girl at heart (grits and sweet tea are their own food group), even though I now live in the northeast. I can sing, well sort of; I meet the biblical requirement. My noise is joyful and unto the Lord. My heart's desire is to live an abundant life, make disciples of all men and establish people in the truth and power of God's Word. My mission is to leave a legacy of love, joy and a deep passion for living in the fullness of the Word of God.

INSPIRED BY LOVE

A Note From Dr. Dawn:

My dear reader…..

Place Your Name Here

It is my hope that something in your heart and your thoughts changed as you read these pages. I know how hard it can be just figuring out who you are and what kind of woman/man you want to be. I know that life can throw blows at you that knock the very wind out of you, confusing every area of your life. But I also know that God made you specifically for your life, this life. He knew how strong you would need to be. He knew how much you could take and He knew that you were going to win. So on the next few pages, I would like for you to share a bit of your journey with the hope that it will encourage and strengthen you to keep going.

As you strategically plan your next move and design your master plan let me ask you……What INSPIRES you?

_____

_____

_____

_____

_____

What are you going to change immediately?

What is your plan to accomplish your goal?

INSPIRED BY LOVE

_____

_____

_____

_____

_____

What would you like to say to yourself about everything that you have survived?

_____

_____

_____

_____

_____

_____

_____

_____

To order additional copies or products:
Please contact:
Unlock Publishing House
6715 Suitland Road
Morningside, MD 20746
701-484-3303

Or visit online at:
www.dawnmharvey.com

E-mail:
info@dawnmharvey.com

To request Dawn M. Harvey to speak as a radio/television personality or at your conference, corporate training, women's fellowship, book club or event, please contact: info@dawnharvey.com

You may also locate **each of the authors** through Facebook or their social media outlets. They are all available for your speaking or training events.

www.ingramcontent.com/pod-product-compliance
Lightning Source LLC
Chambersburg PA
CBHW052026070526
44584CB00016B/1913